W9-AEG-931

Winter Park
PUBLIC LIBRARY

Book-A-Year
Endowment

In memory of

Cynthia E. White

Presented by

Mrs. Edna C. Hayes

PARIS IN LOVE

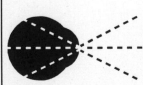 This Large Print Book carries the
Seal of Approval of N.A.V.H.

Paris in Love

A MEMOIR

Eloisa James

THORNDIKE PRESS
A part of Gale, Cengage Learning

GALE
CENGAGE Learning·

Detroit • New York • San Francisco • New Haven, Conn • Waterville, Maine • London

Copyright © 2012 by Eloisa James.
Grateful acknowledgment is made to Random House, an imprint of The Random House Publishing Group, a division of Random House, Inc., and Curtis Brown, Ltd., for permission to reprint "Their Lonely Betters" from *Collected Poems* by W. H. Auden, copyright © 1951 by W. H. Auden.
An early draft of "A Parisian Winter" appeared on the blog One for the Table (www.oneforthetable.com).
Thorndike Press, a part of Gale, Cengage Learning.

ALL RIGHTS RESERVED
Paris in Love is a work of nonfiction. Nonetheless, some of the names and personal characteristics of the individuals involved have been changed in order to disguise their identities. Any resulting resemblance to persons living or dead is entirely coincidental and unintentional.
Thorndike Press® Large Print Nonfiction.
The text of this Large Print edition is unabridged.
Other aspects of the book may vary from the original edition.
Set in 16 pt. Plantin.

LIBRARY OF CONGRESS CATALOGING-IN-PUBLICATION DATA

James, Eloisa.
   Paris in love : a memoir / by Eloisa James.
     pages ; cm. — (Thorndike Press large print nonfiction)
   ISBN-13: 978-1-4104-5164-4 (hardcover)
   ISBN-10: 1-4104-5164-X (hardcover)
   1. James, Eloisa. 2. Authors, American—Biography. 3. Women authors, American—Biography. 4. Americans—France—Paris—Biography. 5. Cancer—Patients—Biography. 6. Life change events. 7. Quality of life—France—Paris. 8. Self-actualization (Psychology) 9. Large type books. I. Title.
   PS3560.A3796Z46 2012b
   813'.54—dc23
   [B]   2012021810

Published in 2012 by arrangement with Random House, Inc.

Printed in Mexico
3 4 5 6 7 16 15 14 13

Paris in Love *is dedicated to my family: to my beloved Alessandro and to my children, Luca and Anna, who unwittingly provided much of the humor in it.*

CONTENTS

AN INTRODUCTION TO
LA VIE PARISIENNE

In December 2007, my mother died of cancer; two weeks later I was diagnosed with the same disease.

I've always been an obsessive reader of memoirs, particularly those that revolve around terrible diseases. While gawking at car accidents gives you a toe-curling sense of shame, perusing a memoir about multiple sclerosis, for example, has an air of virtue — as if by reading about other people's tragedies, you are gathering intelligence about your own possible future. Having read at least ten cancer memoirs before my diagnosis, I was quite sure about what would happen next.

I immediately started anticipating the epiphany when I would be struck by the acute beauty of life. I would see joy in my children's eyes (rather than stark rebellion), eschew caffeine, and simply *be,* preferably while doing yoga in front of a sunset. My better, less irritable self would come out of hiding, and I would stop wasting time at the computer and sniping at my husband.

I have cancer . . . but the good news is that I will learn to live in the moment.

Or perhaps not.

When the Life-Is-Precious response didn't immediately appear, I delayed making joy my modus vivendi while I looked for a doctor. My mother had demanded that her surgeon give her at least enough time to finish her novel-in-progress, and her surgeon had delivered. Mom had the copyedits right there in the hospice with her. I couldn't concentrate on joy when I was obsessively trying to figure out which breast specialist would give me the time I wanted — about forty more years. Maybe fifty.

My sister, Bridget, who is science-minded and capable of retaining unpleasant medical facts, accompanied me on the quest for the right oncologist. We first saw a fierce woman on Madison Avenue who had decorated her office with Wonder Woman dolls. I took this as a sign of somewhat juvenile (but welcome) joie de vivre, but Bridget deemed it too self-congratulatory. Dr. Wonder Woman was ready to battle tremendous odds; her eyes shone with a true-believer fervor as she prescribed removing various parts of my body and radiating much of what was left. She wrestled me onto a cot and drew blood for a gene test right there in her office. "Don't worry about your insurance," she said blithely. "After they hear your family history, they'll pay up."

Once I learned that I didn't have the BRAC gene, the one that brands you with a big red C for cancer, I couldn't get myself to go back to her office. For BRAC carriers, Dr. Wonder Woman offered a scorched-earth policy and the zeal to Fight the Good Fight. I had started sleeping better once I decided that my early-stage case was like herpes, another disease I'd read about and hoped to avoid: disagreeable, but hardly terminal.

Eventually Bridget and I found a calm, quiet oncologist who recommended radiation and hormone treatment, but also noted the salient fact that my breast was the culprit. I stopped thinking about herpes. This was a part of my body that I could live without. In rapid order, I lost that breast.

But having escaped chemotherapy and radiation, did I have the right to call myself a survivor, especially when my newly reconstructed breast turned out to be so pneumatic and round? I decided the answer was no, explaining my lack of epiphany and my

11

disinclination to watch the sun rise from a downward dog position. No pink ribbon for me. Obviously, my diagnosis just wasn't serious enough to change my personality.

Lucky me. I had a better profile but the same old psyche.

And then, without consciously deciding to, I began to shed my possessions. I started with my books. Since I was seven, I had compulsively collected novels, cataloging them and keeping my favorites close to the door in case of fire. My boxed set of The Chronicles of Narnia bore a large sign instructing my parents not to forget it as they carried my (presumably unconscious) body through the door, just before the ceiling fell in.

Now, though, I started giving away books with abandon. My husband, Alessandro, had weathered my bout with cancer with considerably more aplomb than he did its aftermath. As I purged my own belongings, I proselytized the same, but to no effect. Alessandro was flatly uninterested, as anyone might have guessed from the neatly labeled boxes in our attic containing every exam he'd given since 1988. I sometimes worried that the floor might buckle from the tons of Italian literature stored under the eaves. The day he discovered three of his books that I had mistakenly placed in a box labeled Goodwill shall not soon be forgotten in our marriage. It was like our honeymoon night, when he set alight an ornamental fire in our room at the bed-and-breakfast and smoked out all the sleepy guests. That blaze is stuck in my memory, and those three books are stuck in his.

But I didn't stop with books. I did the same with my clothes, jettisoning unopened packages of black stockings from the eighties, the silk nightgown I'd worn on my smoky wedding night, miniskirts in size six. I gave away our wedding presents. My high school term papers hit the recycling bin, followed by college essays and even the children's artwork, which I had once found endlessly endearing.

For years we had talked of living in Manhattan, in the nostalgic fashion with which my mother used to inform me that she might have been a ballerina, if only I had not come along. Alessandro had grown up in an apartment in the center of Florence; he hankered after narrow alleys and the noise of recycling trucks smashing wine bottles at 4:00 A.M. But I grew up on a farm, and when we moved to the East Coast, I had insisted that we live in the suburbs, even though I would be teaching in the city. I thought that parenthood entailed a backyard, a tree, and the sacrifice of urban delights.

So we had settled into a charming house in New Jersey, with a backyard, a mock pear tree, two studies, and forty bookcases. But now, all these years later, lying on the couch recuperating from my surgery, I realized that I had no close friends nearby who might stop in and bring me tea. The people I loved were New Yorkers who braved the bridge and tunnel to bring me certificates for day spas — in the city.

We found a realtor.

Staring out the living room window at that mock pear tree, I also discovered a keen desire to surprise myself. Rather than living *my* life in the moment, I wanted to live someone else's life — specifically, that of a person who lived in Paris. Being a professor has many drawbacks (such as a minuscule salary), but having no time off is not one of them. We could each take a sabbatical year; we simply needed to renew our passports. Once Alessandro found that there was an Italian school in Paris that our bilingual children could attend, I turned my back on the pear tree and bought new drapes for the windows. I filled the empty spots in the denuded bookshelves with pink vases. The

14

house sold in five days, during the worst real estate market in decades. Our cars were last to go.

Luca and Anna, the younger members of our family, were less than enthralled, to say the least, at the prospect of decamping to France. They were particularly struck by the fact that, of all of us, only Alessandro spoke French. (Although they had received good grades for three years in French class, they were right: they couldn't speak the language.) I informed my disbelieving children that inability to understand our neighbors would make their experience more gripping. Threatened with insubordination, I pointed out that I, too, had loathed my parents at their age; instigating fear and mutiny in one's offspring is a parental duty.

Friends were kissed goodbye, Facebooking promises were made, toys were packed. Large amounts of logo-emblazoned clothing were purchased, since a savvy friend promised us that a prominent display of American brands would ensure popularity in the Leonardo da Vinci School.

Paris awaited: a whole year with no teaching and no departmental responsibilities, just *la vie Parisienne.*

In August we moved to an apartment on rue du Conservatoire, a two-block-long street most notable for the music that floats, on warm afternoons, from the open windows of the conservatory. We found ourselves in the 9th arrondissement, in a quartier that is home to various immigrant populations, the Folies Bergère, and more Japanese restaurants than I have fingers.

I had made grand plans to write four books while in Paris: a scholarly book about Jacobean boys' drama in 1607, a couple of romance novels, and a historical novel. But in spite of these inestimable ambitions, I found myself walking for hours. I read books in bed while rain hit the window. Sometimes I spent two weeks doing one Sunday *New York Times* crossword, toiling every night to solve a clue that likely took Will Shortz two seconds to solve.

Soon enough, I discovered an interesting fact: if a writer doesn't put in hours at the keyboard every day, no writing gets done. I had always suspected this was true, but having grown up in a family of writers (and a family without a television at that), I never had the chance to test it out. Even during an inglorious, nonacademic spell after college, I returned home after work to plug away at a novel. Remember, my mother sat in her hospice bed correcting copyedits. Leisure didn't seem to be part of my DNA.

Yet virtually the only writing I did was on Facebook, where I created something of an online chronicle, mirroring it in even more concise form on Twitter. As each day passed, my thumbnail entries fell off the bottom of my Facebook page, relegated to Older Posts. My tweets evaporated, as ephemeral and trivial, as sweet and heedless, as our days in Paris.

A selection of these posts — organized, revised, a few expanded into short essays — has become this book. For the most part, I have retained the short form, the small explosion of experience, as it best gives the flavor of my days.

Those days were organized not around to-do lists and book deadlines but around walks in the park and visits to the fishmonger. Deadlines came and went without a catastrophic blow to my publishing career; I relaxed into a life free of both students and committee work; *laziness* ceased to be a frightening word.

I never did learn how to live in the moment, but I did learn that moments could be wasted and the world would continue to spin on its axis.

It was a glorious lesson.

A Parisian Fall

We spent the summer in Italy, then rented a car and drove to Paris. I pictured this drive as the proverbial "quality time," a charming entrée to a year of creative freedom. But in fact, the children took it as a chance to catch up on missed television, now endlessly available thanks to the Internet. "Look, kids," I shouted from the front seat. "There's a glorious château off to our right!" The only response was wild laughter inspired by *Family Guy* riffs on Ronald Reagan. They weren't even alive for his presidency.

Last night we stayed with friends who own a kiwi orchard in Cigliano, in northern Italy, a misty, dim forest with rows of female trees, heavy with fruit, interspersed with fruitless males. The farmhouse had hooks over the beds to hang drying herbs and sausages. Showing no respect for tradition,

Luca freaked out at the "meat hooks" and begged to be allowed to sleep in the car. We managed to keep from our friends his belief that their beloved house was really a charnel.

Back in the car for the final leg of our journey to Paris, Anna played fart noises on her iPod Touch off and on for hours. I tried to ignore the way my ten-year-old had regressed to half that age and kept my head turned to the window. The French highway was lined with short, vertical pipes from which ferns sprouted. The frilly parts made it look as though the troll dolls from my childhood were hiding in the pipes — perhaps waiting for a chance to hitchhike, if the right family were to happen along.

Our Paris apartment is elegant in the way of a Chanel coat found in an attic trunk: worn around the edges but beautifully designed. The building dates to the 1750s, and the wood floors are all original. The kitchen and bathroom are at the far end of a long corridor that bends around one corner of the building's courtyard — so that the smells (and the servants) would be isolated.

■ ■ ■ ■

Our *gardienne,* it emerged, is not French but Portuguese, with a round face and a bright smile. Alessandro went downstairs with her and was gone for an entire hour; it seems they discussed the price of vegetables the whole time. He reported that store owners on rue Cadet, the shopping street two blocks over, are all thieves. Armed with this knowledge, and dutifully following instructions, we set out for a covered market, Marché Saint-Quentin, where the vegetables are cheaper and the vendors are honorable. We found a dazzling variety of fruit, including four varieties of grapes: small, glistening purple ones, big violet ones, green ones with wild sweetness, and tiny green ones with bitter seeds.

We just spent three hours opening a bank account. I thought our charmingly chatty banker would never stop talking. As he carried on, I felt more and more American. He even gave us a phone number to call for advice *diététique.* French women must not be universally thin if they need dietary advice from their bank.

There is a small hotel across the street from our building, and another to our right. Halfway down the street is an enormous Gothic church called Saint-Eugène–Sainte-Cécile. I gather that Cecilia is the patron saint of music; the conservatory is right next door. Being in the church is like being inside an enameled treasure box that a demented artisan slaved over for years. Every surface — pillars, walls, ceiling — is covered with ornament, most in different patterns. We gaped until we were shooed out, as Mass was going on. I was a bit humiliated about not understanding a word, thinking it was my defective French, but it turned out to be entirely in Latin. We're going to try the American Catholic church instead.

In a wild burst of preparation for ninth grade, Luca has just had his lovely Italian curls straightened. Now he looks like a fifteen-year-old French teen, but with an Italian nose.

Today we joined a Rollerblading event: thousands of hip Parisians zipping over a medieval bridge as the sun shone on the

Seine. Until I ricocheted off a stranger and flopped on my bottom. A race organizer told me sweetly that "eet eez too *difficile*." That, as they say, was that. We fell into café chairs and watched Paris stream by as we drank Oranginas. Then we rode back, slowly, practicing our braking.

This morning I saw a chic French woman in the Métro . . . wearing a beret. How is that possible? I would look unbearably twee, like one of the chipmunks, from *Alvin and the Chipmunks* doing "Singin' in the Rain."

Anna hates Paris. She hates the move, she hates leaving her friends, she hates her new school, she hates everything. I am the only mother in France dragging a child with her nose in a book down the street, the better not to see anything Parisian.

Our apartment has a sweeping staircase, and stained-glass windows looking into the courtyard — and a tiny, slow elevator added in the 1960s. My husband and I both fit in only by standing side by side and sucking in our tummies. Sometimes the groceries fit, too. The children have to take the stairs. I generally emerge to find Anna lying on the last few steps, gasping, one hand outflung toward the (locked) door, doing a great imitation of dying-man-in-desert-sees-mirage.

The butcher down the street has started flirting with me! It makes me feel as though I'm in a movie. He also gave me a one-euro discount on my sausages. Alessandro's unromantic assessment is that the butcher is an excellent marketer. Which is true. I am now a customer for life.

Alessandro was born and grew up in Florence, Italy, with a passion for learning languages (English and Latin in high school, French, German, Russian, and ancient Greek thereafter). When I first met him, he had a charming accent that he shed after having been, as he puts it, seduced into domesticity. He's now a professor of Italian literature at Rutgers University, and was even knighted by the Italian government for obscure intellectual contributions to the republic. At any rate, Alessandro made up his mind not to squander the opportunity to make his French as good as his English, and to that end he's put a notice on an Internet bulletin board offering to exchange an hour of French conversation for an hour of Italian. He's being deluged with responses — most of which seem to be treating his offer as an opportunity for a blind date. My personal favorite is from Danielle ("but some call me Dasha, your choice"), who wrote saying that she had an extra ticket to *The Nutcracker,* and that they would have a great time speaking French, especially after drinking much champagne.

This morning the Thai restaurant at the bottom of our street exploded, resulting in clouds of white smoke and a terrible smell of burning rubber. The *gardienne* came up to the fourth floor to tell us that she thought the owners were doing something nefarious in their basement.

The woman who works in the Italian grocery down the street turns out to be from Alessandro's hometown. Once this interesting fact was established, she took charge of his groceries, removing the olive oil (inferior), switching to buffalo mozzarella (fresher than the kind he'd chosen), and slicing Parma prosciutto rather than San Daniele. It occurs to me that the wily Florentine extracted quite a few more euros from Alessandro's wallet by claiming kinship, but her creamy, delicate mozzarella is worth every penny.

■ ■ ■ ■

It's night, after a day of rain . . . the windows are open and the strains of a glorious opera pour from the conservatory down the street.

Like any big city, Paris has homeless citizens. But I've never before seen a woman carefully sweeping the doorstep where she, her baby, and her husband sleep. Some homeless Parisians have little pup tents and simply flip them open on the street; many have carefully tended cats and dogs on leashes.

Mirabile dictu! Anna has found two things she likes in Paris. The first is chocolate, and the second is the rat catcher's shop, which has four big rats hanging upside down from traps. We detour to gawk at them before grocery shopping.

Archetypal French scene: two boys playing in the street with baguettes were pretending not that they were swords, as I first assumed, but giant penises.

Big excitement! We have just entertained a

fraudulent chimney sweep, ostensibly sent by the landlord's insurance company. He set to work, but Alessandro decided to check up on him. It was all a scam to get us to pay for unneeded cleaning. The sweep had to be thrown out, brushes, rods, and all, with much French protesting and yelping, after cleaning two chimneys. It felt very Dickensian.

Anna has just told me of my demise. She re-created our family in the Sims computer game, and I died after refusing to stop reading in order to eat. "Next time," she said, "I'll make you a rock star, and then you won't mind leaving the house."

At home, meat comes encased in plastic, shiny and shrink-wrapped; the very sight of it reminds me that red meat has been tied to cancer. Here every kind of meat looks fresher than the last. The butcher chars the last feathers from a beautifully plump goose as he lays it before you. At first pigeons reminded me of my office window back in New York; now I see tiny, delicious chickens. The *"bio"* — that is, all-natural — pigeon is particularly enticing.

A wooden pallet is descending silently past

my study window from the floor above, carrying down exquisite furniture: fabulous chairs, a library table, an antique writing desk. This spectacle is terrible for my writing schedule, as I hurtle from my chair every fifteen minutes to ogle.

The Italian school, Leonardo da Vinci, is graced by a nondescript door, but you can easily tell where you are by the flock of Italian *mamma*s standing on the sidewalk, chattering madly about the difficulties of finding good pasta in Paris. Luca came home from his first day of school with a shell-shocked expression. He's expected to do "architectural drawing" (whatever that is), Latin-to-Italian translation, and a kind of math he can't identify. We think it must be advanced geometry.

The American Catholic Church of Paris turns out to be on avenue Hoche, quite a distance from our apartment. Mass is like a sweet time capsule to my 1970s Lutheran Bible camp: lots of guitars, hand-holding, and singing "It only takes a spark to get a fire going . . ."

Between six thirty and seven o'clock in the evening, every other person on the street swings a long baguette partially wrapped in white paper. Suddenly, the world is full of crusty bread.

We are the sometime owners of an obese Chihuahua named Milo, who traveled regularly between the United States and Italy until one fateful August when Air France declared he was too fat to board their plane. Since then he has lived in Florence with Alessandro's mother, Marina, whose cooking has had a further ruinous effect on his waistline. Today Marina called to say that stress has given Milo a few more pounds (although the vet unsympathetically suggested the weight gain was the result of an overindulgence in prosciutto). The source of Milo's stress is hard to pinpoint; among other indulgences, he literally sleeps on a velvet cushion, like an emperor's cat in a fairy tale. But Marina claims that the mere presence of other dogs on the street (and, by extension, in the world) is very upsetting for him.

In a mad rush this morning, I didn't eat, trying to get Anna to school on time. Returning home on the Métro, I struggled out of my coat — only to realize that I was still wearing my pajama top. I stood with blushing ears among elegant commuters for eight stops, too hemmed in to put my coat back on, pretending I wasn't wearing fuzzy green-and-yellow-stripy flannel.

At home, both children attended a Quaker-esque school that specialized in cozy chats as a form of discipline, but here the instructors shriek at kids and make them stand against the wall. Even worse, after only a few days of class, Luca and Anna have realized that they are at the bottoms of their respective grades. The family is in the grip of a dispiriting feeling that their former, much-beloved school taught them to be very nice, but perhaps wasn't quite so successful on the academic front.

Eleven o'clock Sunday morning: a four-piece brass band took over our street corner and played tunes from *My Fair Lady*. We all crowded to the window, and they blew us kisses and requested money to be thrown. The children took great pleasure in doing precisely that.

Anna flung the door of the apartment open after school: "Mom! I was attacked today!" "What happened?" I asked. "A girl named Domitilla slapped me!" Anna said, eyes

30

open very wide. "She said I was screaming in her ear." We chose Anna's former school in New Jersey with an eye toward just this sort of encounter: they devoted a great deal of time to teaching the students to reject violence, studying Mohandas Gandhi and Martin Luther King, and practicing conflict resolution. I inquired hopefully how Anna responded to her first real taste of play-ground aggression. "I slapped her right back," my daughter explained. "My hand just rose in the air all by itself."

I walked into a hair salon yesterday and asked for my customary red highlights; the *coiffeur* snapped: "*Non!* For you, gold. Red is not chic." It's a good thing that our apart-ment is fitted with low-wattage, environ mentally friendly lightbulbs, because strong light turns me into a marigold.

Alessandro has been asked to join the board of the Leonardo da Vinci School. He com-plained pathetically that he was on sabbati-cal and shouldn't have to do committee work, but ended up agreeing to do it. Today there was a welcome-to-school meeting, during which the Italian teacher for Anna's grade suggested that the class was rather undisciplined, which might make them a challenge to teach. The mother of a class-mate stood up and said that her daughter — let's call her Beatrice — had complained that she was told to stop talking. "You cannot tell my daughter to be still," Beatrice's mother scolded. "She will be traumatized by being silenced. I have raised her to freely speak her mind." I thought this sort of pathological insistence on childhood freedom of speech was an American trait. It's rather gratifying to realize that I was wrongly maligning my country.

I have discovered at least one secret of thin French women. We were in a restaurant last night, with a chic family seated at the next table. The bread arrived, and a skinny adolescent girl reached for it. Without missing a beat, *maman* picked up the basket and stowed it on the bookshelf next to the table. I ate more of my bread in sympathy.

Alessandro came home from doing the shopping and said, "I was going to buy you flowers because of the argument we had yesterday." I looked at his empty hands. He shrugged. "There were too many to choose from."

THE EIFFEL TOWER

One October day we picked up Anna and her new friend Erica after school and walked to the Eiffel Tower. The girls ran ahead, zooming here and there like drunk fighter pilots showing off. Alessandro and I tried to imagine why the French ever planned to demolish the tower after the 1889 World Fair. It's such a beautiful, sturdy accomplishment; destroying it would be like painting over the Mona Lisa because of her long nose.

Smallish *bateaux mouches,* or tourist boats, moor in the Seine near the foot of the tower, or so my guidebook said. We wandered beneath the lacework iron, the girls skittering and shrieking like seagulls. Down by the water we paid for the cheaper tickets, the kind that come without crepes and champagne. With twenty minutes to wait, we retreated to an ancient carousel next to the river. A plump woman sat huddled in her little ticket box, shielded from tourists and the rain, although as yet neither had appeared.

Anna and Erica clambered aboard, but still the operator waited, apparently hoping that two children astride would somehow attract more. The girls sat tensely on their garish horses, their skinny legs a little too long. At ten years old, they'll soon find themselves too dignified for such childish amusements. But not yet.

Finally the music started and the horses jerked forward. A crowded merry-go-round on a sunny day is a blur of children's grins and bouncing bottoms. But as the girls disappeared from view, leaving us to watch riderless horses jolt up and down, I realized that an empty merry-go-round on a cloudy day loses that frantic gaiety, the sense that the horses dash toward some joyful finish line.

These horses could have been *objets trouvés,* discovered on a dustheap and pressed into service. The steed behind Anna's was missing the lower half of his front leg.

They arched their necks like chargers crossing the Alps on some military crusade, battle-scarred and mournful. Every chip of gold paint dented by a child's heels stood out, stark and clear.

With nowhere to go, and nothing better to do, the operator let the girls go around and around. Finally, though, the music slowed, the last few notes falling disjointedly into the air.

I decided there is nothing more melancholy than a French carousel on a rainy day, and wished we had paid for champagne and crepes.

On the Métro heading to school, Anna launched into a wicked impersonation of her enraged English teacher stamping her foot: "Shut zee mouths! Zit down! Little cretins!" The entire subway car was laughing, though Anna remained totally unaware of her captive and captivated audience.

Alessandro brought home a very successful makeup present after the non-flowers: a heart-shaped cheese, sort of a Camembert/Brie, as creamy as butter and twice as delicious. We ate it on crusty bread, with a simple salad of orange peppers, and kiwis for dessert.

I just came across a list Luca created on a scrap of paper. At the top of the sheet he wrote (in cursive) "The End." The list is entitled "Several Problems":

- *Can't write in cursive script*
- *Can't write in Italian*
- *Don't think I copied the math homework down correctly*
- *Screwed up on the Italian writing evaluation*
- *Have French essay for Monday*
- *Need my books by tomorrow*

I feel terrible. What have we done, bringing him here? I have ulcers just reading the list.

My sister mentioned before we left for France that a relative on our mother's side had published a memoir about living in Paris. I'd never heard of Claude C. Washburn, who was one of my grandmother's brothers and died before I was born. But today the post brought *Pages from the Book of Paris,* published in 1910. From what I can gather, Claude was born in Duluth, Minnesota, and moved to Europe after getting his undergraduate degree, living in France and Italy. At some point after his year or so in Paris, he married a woman with the unusual name of Ivé. I'm not very far into the book, but so far he has characterized marriage as "an ignominious institution" and boasted of his "increasing exultation" at remaining a bachelor, steering clear of "the matrimonial rocks, that beset one's early progress, toward the open sea of recognized bachelordom." Ivé must have scuppered his vessel before he could steer clear of her rocks.

It started to pour while we were out for dinner, so hard that a white fog hovered above the pavement where the rain was bouncing. We ran all the way home, skittering past Parisians with umbrellas and unprepared tourists using newspapers as cocked hats, the water running down our necks, accompanied by an eight-block-long scream from Anna.

Today I went to my favorite flirtatious butcher and pointed to some sausages. He coiled up seven feet of them and put them on the scale, saying, "The man who is married to you needs to eat lots of sausages." One problem with my French is that I require time to think before replying, so I ended up back out on the street with far too many sausages and spent the next hour unsuccessfully trying to come up with French ripostes that I will be able to use in my next life. The one in which I am fluently multilingual, and never at a loss for words.

■ ■ ■ ■

Anna had to stand against the wall twice during one class period yesterday. I asked her why, and she told me that she couldn't remember, and anyway, she wasn't as bad as the boys. I can't wait for parent-teacher conferences. "She's a bad American" keeps running through my head to the tune of "She's a very pretty girrrrlll . . ."

My favorite of Paris's many bridges is Pont Alexandre III, and my favorite of its many statues is not one of those covered with gold, but rather a laughing boy holding a trident and riding a fish. Although just a child, he's bigger than I am, his huge toes flying off the fish as he twists in midair. But he's a boy still, with a guileless smile — caught in a moment when he is big enough to ride the back of a fish but not yet acquainted with the world's sorrows and deceits. On the far end of Pont Alexandre III, opposite the mer-boy, sits his twin sister. She seems to have just left the water; she holds fronds of seaweed in one hand, and in the other a large seashell to her ear. Her face is intent as she looks into the distance, listening carefully. I imagine that she is listening for the rushing sound of waves, the sound of home.

Every Peter Pan has his Hook, Harry Potter his Malfoy . . . Anna's nemesis is Domitilla, the young lady who slapped her on the playground. Domitilla is a talkative Italian with a propensity for hogging the spotlight (which Anna prefers to reserve for herself). "She is devilish," Anna told me, very seriously, this morning on the way to school.

"We'd like white wine," Alessandro tells our wine seller, Monsieur Juneau. "What are you eating?" M. Juneau inquires. "Fish." "What kind of fish?" "Halibut with mint and lemon," I report. "And on the side?" "Potatoes." "Small or large?" asks Monsieur. (Who knew *that* mattered?) "Small." Our menu rolls off his tongue, sounding like the *carte du jour* at a three-star Michelin restaurant. "The wine for you," he says, lovingly plucking down a bottle. At home, the fish is disastrous, but the wine, a revelation.

Luca has caught a virus, and declared pathetically this morning that there was only one thing in the world he could bring himself to eat: Froot Loops. I picked up Anna at school, and we detoured to a small store called the Real McCoy, which caters to homesick American expats. Jackpot! We bought brown sugar, marshmallows, and Froot Loops. Luca ate three bowls.

Ballerinas fall out of the conservatory on our street, eager for a smoke. They cluster around the steps, hip bones jutting. Today, two of them are resplendent in pink tutus, absentmindedly stretching their hamstrings.

I worked hard this afternoon on *A Kiss at Midnight,* my reimagining of *Cinderella.* My heroine is flat-chested, poor thing, and part of her transformation involves a pair of "bosom friends" made of wax. These accoutrements are thoroughly historical, and great fun to write about. I gave her so many misadventures that I felt very glad to have gone through with reconstruction surgery, so I don't have to walk around wearing a wax tata.

Today Alessandro had his first meeting with a Frenchman from the "conversation exchange" website. His name is Florent, and he wants to learn Italian because he bought a plot of land in a tiny village near Lucca, in Tuscany, and he plans to build a house there. But mostly because he is in love with a waitress he met in the village. Apparently she is very, very shy and reserved.

We woke this morning to a sheet of rain pouring into the street, with the kind of concentrated intensity that made me think, drowsily, that our bedroom could be behind a waterfall: a dim and cool cave, our big windows a pane of moving water.

Today Anna was kicked out of her math class and sent to the hallway to "think about herself." I asked her what she thought about. In lieu of self-examination, she planned a new Sims family, but admitted that she was afraid I would kill her before she got to make it.

A concerned friend has just written from England to inform me that her son's economics reading included the fact that 650 Parisians are hospitalized every year due to dog-poo-related accidents. After living here for almost two months, I am not surprised by this datum. The good news is that we are not (yet) among the fallen.

I walked home at dusk, and everyone I passed was munching a baguette. The pavement looked as if hundreds of lost children had scattered crumbs so they could find their way home again.

Anna's archrival, Domitilla, just returned from her grandmother's funeral in Italy. Apparently Domitilla glanced above the coffin and saw Jesus suspended in the air. Anna's comment: "I was pretty surprised to hear that." But another classmate, Vincenzo, chimed in and said that he knew about a boy with no legs at all who went to church and prayed, and after seeing a white-bearded man in the air, got up and walked. "So that was better than just seeing Jesus," Anna pointed out.

My publisher is in town on her way to the Frankfurt Book Fair, and she took me to lunch at Brasserie Lipp, where Simone de Beauvoir and Jean-Paul Sartre used to lunch every day. I had a dark, delicious fish soup and too much wine; we talked about food, writing and life before children.

People kiss all the time here: romantically, sadly, sweetly, passionately; in greeting and farewell. They kiss on the banks of the Seine, under bridges, on street corners, in the Métro. I hadn't realized that Anna had noticed until yesterday, when I suggested perhaps a single-mother situation in her classroom could be explained by divorce. Anna didn't agree. "They don't get divorced over here," she reported. "It's 'cause they kiss so much."

Very early in the morning, the only light comes from tightly closed bakeries. Chairs are upside down on top of the tables, but the smell of baking bread feels like a welcome.

CHASTISED BY DIOR

I attended Madison Public Elementary School wearing only dresses. No matter how deep the snow, my sister and I stripped off our snow pants in the school hallway to reveal wool tights. In our mother's eyes, we were young ladies, and ladies wore dresses, along with white gloves to church, hats on Easter, and long flannel nightgowns to bed.

She generally sewed those dresses from Simplicity patterns, whose packets featured illustrations of hyperattenuated girls with freakishly long legs. Those pattern packets would float around the house, the jaunty hip-hugging belt in matching plaid never looking quite as good in my mother's rendition. By the time I was ten years old, I was prone to fits of deep sartorial lust. Even all these years later, I can still remember certain articles of clothing that I longed for in 1974. My classmate Rachel Larson has undoubtedly forgotten the matching jacket and jeans she wore to the first day of school in fourth grade.

I have not.

It wasn't until my entrance into middle school that I was allowed to buy exotic contraband — trousers, in the form of a pair of burnt orange bell-bottom corduroys. Perhaps unsurprisingly, it's occurred to me recently that I'm close to fifty and I'm still wearing a version of those bell-bottoms.

When I'm teaching, I wear a female approximation of men's business clothing, down to the lace-up shoes. Without an audience to consider, though, I sacrifice fashion for warmth, pulling on fur lined clogs, my cords, silk camisoles edged with lace that peeks from the neck of whatever large sweater I'm wearing. I formed this pattern in my twenties, when a provocative flash of lace was, well, provocative. It doesn't feel sensual or remotely fashionable these days, but I live with it.

Most of the fourth grade of the Leonardo da Vinci School takes communion class together, at a church in the most chic shopping area of Paris. One day in September I left Anna to her spiritual pursuits and began my own, wandering down avenue Montaigne, past the windows of Dior, Fendi, Lacroix, and Gaultier.

45

The windows of Dior were particularly entrancing. I actually turned back, retracing my steps to look once more at a dress of grave violet silk with a knife-edge pleated skirt and wide looped trim of the same color around the neck. The mannequin came alive in my imagination. I could picture a sleek and gorgeous woman drifting into a drawing room — although she then regarded reproachfully my scuffed shoes and the smudged cuff of my white shirt.

Glancing down, I discovered I was wearing one of Alessandro's countless black sweaters, so bulky that I had a pregnancy-like bulge in the front. I hastily buttoned up my coat. My shoes were the menswear type, comfortable for long walks. I was wearing bell-bottom cords, and I wasn't entirely sure I had put on any makeup.

On the way back to the church, I realized that the streets were crowded with Parisian women in their forties and fifties who would no more think of allowing lacy trim to show under a man's sweater than they would contemplate renting *Flashdance*. They tapped briskly past me in their high-heeled black boots, scarves tied with exquisite finesse, coats snugly hugging their bodies.

Just like that, all the frustrated lust I felt for Rachel Larson's jaunty pantsuit flooded back. The elegance of that Dior mannequin, her effortless insouciance, the turn of her plastic chin and the twist of her plastic wrist, made her haute couture seem just as tantalizingly unavailable.

It has taken most of October, loitering on avenue Montaigne during Anna's weekly hour of spiritual education to gaze at mannequins in designer silks, but I've come up with a New Year's resolution: I want to know what elegance looks like at age fifty, a milestone that looms just a few years away.

I refuse to find myself in my second half century still wearing my furry shoes and Alessandro's sweaters. I intend to learn precisely what these French women buy and, perhaps just as important, how they manage to look so commandingly elegant after attaining *"un certain âge."* It is truly a pity that my mother is no longer alive.

I've finally decided to dress like a lady.

Yesterday Anna announced that she and her babysitter saw an "angry mob storming the street." I made a mental note that Alessandro should cut back on the nightly Dickens readings, but then I read about the strike: apparently, to protest grain prices, farmers threw hay bales into the Champs-Élysées — and set them on fire. This does suggest a certain level of malcontent.

I walk through the streets and enjoy listening to wild chatter in French with the same level of understanding that one has hearing a row of sparrows crowded on a telephone line. Are these people really talking, or are they just singing to each other? They look far too elegant and sophisticated to be uttering the half-assed things people say to each other in New York.

French chickens come with heads and feet still attached . . . my butcher cradles the bird like a baby, then waggles its head toward Anna, turning the bird into a clucking version of *Jaws.*

Paris is enlarging my waistline, and thus I've made the decision that I have to jog. Wanting to make sure I was properly kitted out before this event, I took a few weeks to acquire an iPod, a pair of running shoes, a hat, and a sweatshirt. This morning, out of excuses, I forced myself into the crisp autumn air as Leonard Cohen crooned through my earphones about goodbyes. Seven entire minutes of virtue! My ambitions are not huge.

■ ■ ■ ■

By happenstance, Alessandro encountered Luca's architectural drawing teacher today and inquired how the class was going. Not well. Apparently Luca hasn't turned in a shred of homework since the semester began. "He's such a nice boy," she told Alessandro. "I know he sees the other children hand in their homework, but he never does so himself." This evening Luca said, quite reasonably, that since he had no idea how to do an architectural drawing, he didn't try. He was less successful at explaining why he hadn't mentioned this salient fact to us.

Last night I asked Alessandro if he ever lies in bed and thinks about chocolate — say, about the way dark chocolate feels in your mouth, or how different it is when spiked with orange peel. He said no. Then he said that the only time he thinks about food in bed is when he wakes up in the middle of the night and wants steak. Somewhere in that clash lies a profound truth about the difference between the sexes.

Today I met Anna after school and she

reported that it was a "great day." "Wow," I said, "what happened?" "I didn't get yelled at," she said proudly. And then, "Well, maybe in one class." She is wire-thin, with flyaway blond hair and a single dimple. She doesn't look like someone who has intimate knowledge of principals' offices on two continents.

I walked through the twilight to Galeries Lafayette, surely one of the most glamorous department stores in the world. Far above the cosmetics counters on the grand main floor, a domed stained-glass ceiling shimmers like an enormous kaleidoscope. Instead of a counter, the skin-care company La Mer has a nine-foot-long sinuous aquarium. Dolce & Gabbana has its own little salon, with chandeliers made of black glass blown into elegant, slightly sinister, shapes.

Quelle horreur! The *gardienne* came to clean and noticed that our glassware was smeared, which has been driving me crazy. The box of dishwashing powder that we'd been using? Salt! It looked like dishwashing powder, it was under the sink, and I never bothered to puzzle out the label. We have been running the dishwasher with salt alone for two months.

■ ■ ■ ■

Last night we trotted out to our local Thai
"gastronomique" restaurant, which means it's
a trifle more fancy than average and serves
mango cocktails. A man and his son came
in, trailed by a very old, lame golden re-
triever. The dog felt like lying down, legs
straight out, in the middle of the aisle running down the restaurant — on a Friday
night. The waiter and all customers patiently
stepped over and around him, over and over
and over . . . Bravo, France!

It's raining. Our neighborhood homeless
man hasn't moved from where he sits on
the sidewalk, next to the Métro stop, but he
cocked one big umbrella over himself, a
smaller one over his dog, and a third over
his belongings. The umbrellas look like
wildly colorful mushrooms sprouting from
the pavement. From down the street, they
seem to bloom, low and colorful against the
gray buildings.

Alessandro and Luca sat down at the dining
room table after school and wrestled with
Luca's architectural drawing homework.
After what seemed to be a great deal of
exertion, they brandished a complicated

looking plan, replete with circles and arrows and lines in all directions. "How on earth did you do it?" I asked. "We mostly copied it from the book," Alessandro admitted. I practiced wifely virtue and didn't say anything about professorial views of plagiarism.

One of Alessandro's friends from college, Donatella, is attached to the Italian Cultural Institute here. It's her birthday, so we're going to dinner at Ladurée, a restaurant on the Champs-Élysées that was founded in the 1800s. They are famous for their patisserie, which made the pastel-colored *macarons* for Sofia Coppola's film *Marie Antoinette.* We're planning to dress to the nines and drink a lot of champagne.

Anna, looking at my Facebook fan page: "Can you switch that picture?" "Yes," I say. "Then why don't you put me there?" "You? Why would I put you there?" "Because I'm your Mini-Me. I just need some glasses and no one would know." A point of fact: she just turned eleven, she's blond, and she weighs about four pounds. I'm forty-seven, a redhead, and weigh considerably more.

At Ladurée, I had fabulous fish with ginger fennel. The only disappointment, oddly enough, was the dessert, chosen from a ten-page menu. We read every single offering, and I finally chose a rum cake. It was soggy and arrived in a plastic cup, so it had the general aura of coming from an inebriated vending machine. Ladurée's own brand of rosé champagne went some way toward amelioration.

We walked past a group of Parisian teen-agers laughing boisterously in the street, and Alessandro pointed out that we never laugh like that anymore. These days happiness is quieter, captured perhaps in one of the kids laughing, or the bliss of hearing a favorite song when I actually have time to listen to it.

It's school break, so I took Anna and her friend Nicole to the Marais. We had brunch at Des Gars dans la Cuisine, a chic little restaurant on rue Vieille-du-Temple with large, low windows lined with red-cushioned window seats. The girls had hamburgers, gussied up with a touch of nouvelle cuisine. With great kindness, the waitress brought out little pots of applesauce for them. Unfortunately, the moment she turned her back they declared scornfully that apple-sauce was for babies, so I had to eat both pots so that the waitress would not feel snubbed.

Our children are driving us mad. As a surprise, Alessandro came home today with train tickets for London, dated tomorrow. Apparently it's only about two hours by Eurostar, through the Channel Tunnel.

The Eurostar that runs between London and Paris has full security; consequently, we almost missed the train. We collapsed into our seats and then spent a lively two hours as the children battled over one copy of *Diary of a Wimpy Kid,* regardless of the fact they'd both read it several times. In a low moment, a jostled arm led to an airborne flood of hot tea landing on Alessandro's pants in just such a spot as to suggest that he needs Depends. This led to the revelation that he brought only that pair for the next three days.

In the late afternoon we set out for Big Ben. But it was rush hour in the Underground, and we finally fled the crowd. We got lost in a big park, a helicopter hovering overhead. Alessandro thought he recognized Buckingham Palace, but it turned out to be the back of an apartment building. We were all making fun of him when we saw a motorcycle cop zoom by ahead, and then another one. Alessandro started running toward the street, shouting, "The Queen!" We all ran after him, laughing hopelessly and shouting insults. But he was right! Her Majesty Elizabeth II was riding along in a Rolls-Royce, bolt upright, a dorky scarf tied securely under her chin. This was a highlight of our trip, though the children were truly impressed only after a taxi driver confided that he hadn't seen her in eleven years of driving.

We had a long, fractious lunch punctuated by battles over the one functioning iPod Touch, and then went to Harrods, where we bought a Christmas pudding and wandered through women's designer clothing. Anna fell in love with fur. I pulled her away from rubbing her cheek against the minks. "It's so soft," she said dreamily. "Just like my hair in the morning after I wash it."

Everyone's favorite exhibit at the Victoria & Albert Museum was the Great Bed of Ware, which apparently sleeps eighteen — though not if they're American, we decided after much discussion. In the gift shop, Luca bought a shaggy hat with little sheep horns. He's all hair these days. The saleslady said,

"I was watching you decide. . . . He had to have this. It's an extension of himself."

Best bit of history from yesterday: noticing that the big red Royal Mail postboxes have slots for both stamped mail and franked mail. Back in the day, lords could simply sign letters in the area where a stamp might be, and the letters went out for free. . . . I can't believe that's still the case, but it was very exciting to see the slot.

Lunch at Gordon Ramsay's Boxwood Café was wonderful. I had a delicate leek and pea tart, and then sublime crusty black bream, a kind of fish I'd never heard of before. I was torn between "spotted dick" and "fool" for dessert, both less for their intrinsic appeal than for that of their names. Alessandro lowered himself to note that I had enough of the first at home, so I went for the fool. (And virtuously refrained from the obvious retort.)

Life after Gordon is dismal. We went to a celebrated restaurant in the West End . . . but nothing measured up. We all ate mournfully, and Anna made up her own song, the chorus of which was "Pinkberry, blueberry, vomit."

■ ■ ■ ■

In honor of my characters (who have done the same), we had tea and scones in Fortnum & Mason. My favorite moment was in the bathroom, where Anna was happily trying out the lotion. A very nice lady explained to us that "this is the way the posh live every day . . . all the time."

The British are vehicle-mad. We arrived at this conclusion based on seeing two demonstrations: first, a parade of growling, honking Hells Angels–type motorcycle riders protesting a tax on parking. And then, about an hour later, a parade of tiny minicars, not protesting anything, just enjoying being small.

Completely exhausted by cultural and touristic activities, we retreated to Waterstone's bookstore. The hour or two spent there was lovely. No squabbling, no screaming, no whining, just happy heads bent over books. We staggered out with three bags of books — and only one sticky moment, when we were at the counter and Anna's pile turned out to include *My Dad's in Prison*. Alessandro objected.

■ ■ ■ ■

On the Eurostar back to Paris, we assembled a list of fabulous food: Gordon Ramsay's sweet and silky leek tart for me, and his butternut squash and sage risotto for Anna. From a restaurant whose name I can't remember, a pear poached in Armagnac and then baked into a delicate little custard. Plus a Cornish pasty, the one item on this list that I think I can't reproduce.

Anna is dutifully doing homework in the next room — watching *Les Aristochats.* It's so funny to hear the kittens even more Frenchified, not to mention my favorite goose, Abigail, who has been transformed into Amélie.

This apartment came with two small refrigerators, one for food, and one for beverages. The one for food just died. I can push a cauliflower onto the second shelf of the beverage fridge, but it makes the top shelf topple.

Alessandro's conversation-exchange partner, Florent, said today that he doesn't understand Italian women, as the object of his affection is so reserved that he has no idea whether he is moving too fast. If she were a French woman, he says, they would already have had a whole relationship, from first kiss to divorce. Apparently French women kiss first and talk later; Alessandro told Florent that's the pattern of an Italian male. He doesn't think Florent took the hint, though.

I feel taller every day. This morning I crammed onto a rush-hour train only to discover a very petite Frenchman with his head in my armpit. I had to reach over him to hold on to the bar, and we both stood stiff and embarrassed.

I need to work on developing a new, less irritable personality. Though I suspect that an empty nest would be at least a partial cure, today I resorted to substance abuse. I sallied forth to La Grande Epicerie on rue de Sèvres and bought three different kinds of chocolate: Zanzibar's *oranges en robe* (twists of rind with delicious coating), Côte d'Or's *citron gingembre* (a bar with ginger and lemon peel), and Michel Cluizel's *noir aux écorces d'orange* (a dark bar with tiny chunks of orange).

Anna and I had a tasting test. The winner

was Cluizel's *chocolat noir.* It's astounding: deep and rich, with a silky melt.

We have reached a new academic low: Anna brought home a warning note from her Italian teacher about her misbehavior. Rather than being repentant, she was excited by the fact that one of her other teachers had whacked an even naughtier child with a book. We are a nonspanking household, somewhat to Alessandro's disgust (he thinks he turned out the better for his mother's corporal discipline). The sheer novelty of seeing an adult lose her temper and respond in a physical manner fascinated Anna. After signing the note, as requested, I have to admit to a surge of acute sympathy for the teachers managing Anna, Domitilla, and what sounds like a berserking horde of ten-year-old boys.

I ran for all of ten minutes today, a new record. My flirtatious butcher was unloading boxes as I jogged past, and blinked at me, probably startled to see me in Lycra. He has long sideburns, the kind you never see in the United States. I wiggled my fingers at him as I trotted by, and then felt painfully self-conscious about my bottom.

■ ■ ■ ■

In an art gallery: tiny, ornate reliquary boxes, the kind that house a saint's finger bone. But these contain *objets trouvés,* the relics of saints we haven't heard about — my favorite is "Saint Protecteur" (a condom in its jaunty wrapper).

Anna reported today that Domitilla's gerbil died, an event that should instinctively raise a spark of sympathy rather than raucous laughter . . . but no. The gerbil fell off the balcony, and then a flowerpot fell on it, after which its eye bulged out (a gory detail of particular interest). Maybe Anna will be a biologist one day. Or a mortician.

My kitchen window looks down into the courtyard, giving me a view of the couple two stories below. The wife seems to spend her evenings canoodling with a small dog, though she and her husband may have a passionate life hidden from those who peer down into the courtyard, spying into their windows. One could not call her chic, exactly, but she is a French sixty, which means that her hair is always perfect and her eyebrows are plucked to perfection.

61

■ ■ ■ ■

We had a very painful family dinner last night. Luca is pretty sure that he is doing well in his English language and literature class (not much to applaud about there), but is also quite certain that he's failing all his other courses. He doesn't understand math in Italian and believes that the math they're doing doesn't exist in the States (we contested this). He was pretty good at English-to-Latin translation at home, but Latin into a complicated Italian past tense is another story. The kids in his French class have French mothers, which explains why they are reading Voltaire although he is at the Captain Underpants stage. We decided to find tutors. In everything. Maybe even in parenting.

When I wander out, the sky is blue and far away. By the time I emerge from the market, pearl gray clouds seem within my reach. The sidewalk is rain-splattered, and the puppy belonging to the homeless man at our Métro stop retreats under his blanket, nothing showing but a little black nose. I put a euro in the cup and hope it goes to dog food rather than cognac.

■ ■ ■ ■

Today I made gingerbread, only to discover at a crucial point that I had no molasses. I poured in pomegranate molasses instead, since that's the only molasses I've found in Paris. Anna loved it, but Luca wrinkled his nose and said, "Something's missing." Maybe he'll win the palate contest on *Hell's Kitchen* someday.

"You know Domitilla's gerbil that got squished?" Anna asked by way of greeting, after school. "*Well*, Domitilla just threw it away. Right in the trash can. And do you want to know about her other gerbil?" "Sure," I said untruthfully. "She couldn't throw it away because it got lost in the house and died somewhere. So now it's going to smell. She is *really* not good with pets."

My study looks directly onto the gray slanted roofs on the other side of rue du Conservatoire. I love watching rain pour over the slate, creating dark rivers that sheet down the gutters. The cat who lives opposite, whose owner puts her out on the little balcony when she cleans the apartment, is not so enthusiastic about rain.

I just took leftover cauliflower and potato soup, added frozen baby peas and a splash of Thai coriander sauce, threw it all in the blender, and came out with a fabulous soup. Bright green, not to mention healthy, and the children ate every drop.

Marina has put Milo on a diet. Chihuahuas are supposed to weigh about seven pounds, and Milo is more than twenty-seven. He looks like a 1950s refrigerator: low-slung, blocky, and rounded off at the corners. Apparently the vet has suggested vegetables, so for dinner Milo is having lightly steamed broccoli tossed in just a touch of butter, and some diet dog food steeped in home-made chicken broth.

Anna burst out with questions on the Métro today: Do you remember when your boobs started growing? How old were you? Were you fifty? Do your boobs keep growing until you die? I didn't dare glance around to see how many English speakers might be in the car with us.

Around seven o'clock, the autumn light turns clear and bluish, the color of skim milk. All the waiters lean on the doors of their restaurants, smoking, waiting for customers.

THE ROBIN-ANTHEM

In a single week in November, I mixed up *immanent* with *imminent, paramount* with *tantamount,* and *soap* with *soup.* I addressed my friend Philip as "Paris," and I put a roll of paper towels in the dishwasher, rescuing it in the nick of time.

In the middle of the night, I came to the stark conclusion that my brain must be dying. Words are my stock-in-trade; they are my daily bread. In the dark, it seemed obvious that turning Philip into Paris implied I had picked up a hitchhiking brain tumor. Or (thanks to an article I'd recently read in *The New York Times*), Huntington's disease. In the morning, I succumbed to the siren song of Google and typed in "Huntington's."

The Mayo Clinic's website specializes in reassuring language; I quickly gathered that unless and until I started dropping teacups, I was in no danger of that particular diagnosis. Then, just as I was relaxing, I happened on this cheery little passage: "Deciding whether to be tested for the gene is a personal decision. For some people, the uncertainty of whether they carry the faulty gene is stressful and distracting. For others, the knowledge that they will develop the condition is burdensome."

Burdensome? My first reaction was a snort. I'm finding the knowledge of my hopefully not imminent (or immanent) death burdensome, and I don't even have a gene to warn me of that rendezvous. But a moment later I realized that I'm a fool to quibble with the Mayo Clinic's definition of a "faulty gene." Along with the rest of humankind, I inherited faulty genes, *all* of which are programmed to die. It's the knowledge thereof that's tricky.

When I was young I used to lie in bed at night memorizing poetry. Ours was a poetry-infused household, and I a dutiful oldest daughter. I memorized D. H. Lawrence's ode to a snake, loving the sound as he "trailed his yellow-brown slackness soft-bellied down." I never shared my memorized verses with anyone, especially not my poet father. He seemed to have a thousand poems, even more, stockpiled in his brain. He would erupt at dinner with a bit from

King Lear, and then follow up with two quatrains of Blake, and a verse in Swedish. My ambitions were secret and modest by comparison: I wanted a few poems, just a few. I wanted to have those particular words available, to know that Coleridge's river Alph runs "through caverns measureless to man / Down to a sunless sea" and that Frost's snowy forest offered a challenge to those "with promises to keep."

When I went to college I stopped memorizing poetry, thinking that I would pick it up again when I had more time. But as I lay in the dark thinking about how *soup* foamed into *soap,* it occurred to me that I may not have world enough and time to memorize the rest of even a very small canon. My grandmother was diagnosed with dementia, and was silent the last decade of her life; my father, my darling father of a thousand poems and more, has taken to watching leaves fall from their trees. Rather than knit those leaves into words, he simply allows them to fall. It's a cruel fate: to watch without recounting the fall of the leaf; to grieve without creating anew; to age without describing it.

In the last year, as I've watched him struggle with the way age is stealing his words, it occurred to me that I should

68

memorize some more poetry, as ballast against my possible inheritance of that good, wordless night. Here, in its entirety, is the poem with which I resumed my memorization: W. H. Auden's "Their Lonely Betters."

As I listened from a beach-chair in the
    shade
To all the noises that my garden made,
It seemed to me only proper that words
Should be withheld from vegetables and
    birds.

A robin with no Christian name ran
    through
The Robin-Anthem which was all it knew,
And rustling flowers for some third party
    waited
To say which pairs, if any, should get
    mated.

Not one of them was capable of lying,
There was not one which knew that it
    was dying
Or could have with a rhythm or a rhyme
Assumed responsibility for time.

Let them leave language to their lonely
    betters

Who count some days and long for
   certain letters;
We, too, make noises when we laugh or
   weep:
Words are for those with promises to
   keep.

On the Métro, Anna pointed out a tiny
orange ladybug in the car with us. We
watched as she gamely walked upside down
across the ceiling and then flew to the ledge
above the door. As the subway stopped, I
toppled her into my hands and we brought
the ladybug up a flight of stairs, down a
hallway, up two more smaller sets of
stairs . . . finally into the chilly morning,
where she flew into a cluster of glossy
bushes.

Anna and I are slowly exploring the grocery
stores in the Japanese quarter of Paris. My
favorite has a wall of different soy sauces
and an upstairs room filled with mysterious
foods in exotic packaging. Nothing is labeled in French or English, and we bring
things home and puzzle over them.

Alessandro and I followed an exquisite pair
of legs out of the Métro today. They were
clad in flowery black lace stockings and dark

red pumps. Their owner wore a coat with five buttons closing the back flap, and gloves that matched her pumps precisely. We walked briskly up the steps, and I turned around to see the front of the coat, only to find that the lady in question was at least seventy. She was both dignified and *très chic.* Old age, *à la parisienne!*

Twelve teens from Luca's ninth-grade class were out sick today; the H1N1 virus has hit the Leonardo da Vinci High School hard. Luckily, both my kids had got it back in the States, in June. Luca has the same happy glow in his eyes that I used to get while standing at the window watching snowflakes fall in rural Minnesota: will it, will it, *will it* snow enough to close school? The contemporary equivalent involves refreshing Facebook every five minutes, asking friends if they feel feverish, and hoping desperately (disgracefully) that they do, so that the whole school closes down.

All the buildings lining rue du Conservatoire are constructed of cream marble or limestone. When I went outside today, the sky was pale and fierce, on the very cusp of rain. From the top of the church and the conservatory, the contrast was almost imperceptible, as if marble and air danced cheek to cheek.

I just sent Anna to school with a blotted, misspelled, blood-sweat-and-tears note of apology to her teacher for cheating "a little bit" during an exam. She vehemently protested, telling me that her teacher wouldn't care, and that it was like writing a letter to Santa Claus apologizing for burning his beard. The logic of the burning beard escaped me, so I just kept saying, "Your teacher has to sign this letter, Anna."

Last night we went to a bistro gifted with an irritable waiter who brought us tepid skate swathed in salty capers. The menu included a section *à l'ancienne,* so I chose a unique appetizer: beef snout. It came in little strips, drowned in vinaigrette. The taste? Spam! I know Spam because my father was in World War II and would occasionally have a fit of nostalgia and buy some. And now I know what's inside Spam, too.

Halfway through an enormous antiques fair, we collapsed into a tiny café overlooking gardens near the Bastille and drank glasses of *chocolat à l'ancienne* — old-fashioned hot chocolate with whipped cream, topped with a drunk cherry. There was almond laced in there somewhere . . . it was incantatory. As we sat, savoring our chocolate, the atmosphere turned to *l'heure bleue,* the sliver of time between afternoon and evening, when the sky is periwinkle.

Two objects at the antiques fair kept me awake last night, and I had to remind myself several times that possessions don't lead to happiness. The first was a madly improbable Venetian blown-glass chandelier. It was festooned with tiny glass fruit and flowers, and probably dated from the 1950s, taking a crazed glassblower two years of his life. The second was an 1850s mirror, also from Italy. It was framed in black walnut, inlaid with elaborate curlicues and etchings of joyful, inebriated cupids.

The French walk slowly. They amble down the street, meet friends and spend two minutes kissing, then plant themselves, chatting as if the day were created for this moment. My husband and I walk like New Yorkers: fast, dodging obstacles, glancing at windows, going places. It's taken a few months . . . but I now keep thinking: Where am I going that's so urgent, when all these

French people don't agree?

We have migrated from the charming but crowded American church to Saint-Eugène–Sainte-Cécile right on rue du Conservatoire. It turns out that they have a Mass in French as well as the one in Latin (not that it matters to me in terms of comprehension). The priest has nine male acolytes of different ages; incense and little chiming bells are waved around as if they were magic potions guaranteed to increase piety.

We discovered yesterday that our beloved covered market, not to mention the local fishmonger and butcher, is closed on Monday, which left our cupboard bare. For lunch I had a hunk of an excellent Camembert, with a boiled potato sprinkled with coarse sea salt, followed by a leftover apricot tart. Life is good.

Florent, Alessandro's conversation partner, is going to Italy for a visit, so today they practiced romantic phrases. Florent is going to try to move past cheerful commentary. In Italian, you say *"Ti amo"* ("I love you") only to a lover. To everyone else — children, parents, friends — you say *"Ti voglio bene,"* which roughly means "I wish you well." It's very romantic to save *I love you* only for affairs of the heart.

When it rains on rue du Conservatoire, rainwater pours into subterranean conduits that run underneath the sidewalk. The water rushing through those pipes turns drain holes to tiny fountains, squirting rain a few inches into the air. It's as if huge clams were signaling that they were digging deeper, under the streets of the 9th arrondissement.

Yesterday we bought little cans of dog food for "our" homeless man, or rather for his puppy, which is growing very fast and developing the awkward paws that promise he will be a large dog. Anna delivered the first can on her way to school. The puppy knows us now, and leaps from his box with a squeaky bark as soon as we get close. He's a licker, a face licker (of course Anna gets down on his level), but very sweet all the same.

BHV is a huge Paris department store, five floors of everything from lamps to kids' undies and bright pink whisks. I just spent hours there, ending up in the art materials department, where I bought a book of delicate papers from around the world: paper that has designs sewn on it in gold thread, Japanese tissue paper, papers with wild swirls and elegant fleurs-de-lis. Rather than sending a Christmas card depicting the children smiling under duress, I am determined that we will make our own cards this year.

Anna came home with a big grin and told me that Domitilla had a "time of stress" at the blackboard in math class, as the teacher not only shouted, but pounded his fist on the desk. The truth is that I am failing to instill compassion in this child. I talked to her for five minutes about patience, kindness, and generosity, and then she laughed like a hyena and ran away.

I lived in Paris once before, during a junior year abroad. Back then, I was working as a model, which meant that I reflexively averted my eyes from all sorts of culinary temptations. Instead, I salivated over lingerie stores displaying delicate pleated bras and extravagant silk panties. Now I zip past those stores, only to linger at chocolate shops displaying edible chess sets, or a model of Hogwarts in dark chocolate. It's nice that life is long enough to give you desires of many kinds.

This afternoon the doorbell rang, and Alessandro spied our local pharmacist standing down below, in the street. Anna has chronic kidney disease and must take four medications a day, so my instant panic was that there'd been some sort of mix-up. But no. He cheerily said hello, then noted that there was a tiny change in one of her prescriptions, and he wanted to check that we knew (we did). He had hopped across the street just to make sure.

Alessandro feels that he's not speaking enough French, because his conversation partner, Florent, spends most of his free time in Italy wooing the elusive waitress. So today he started another such exchange, this one with a woman named Viviane. She is a professor of American culture, which means that I would essentially be a walking re-search project for her — particularly as she is writing an article on Americans' use of social networks such as Facebook, and I spend an inordinate amount of time fashion-ing my updates.

We took a boat down the Seine today and saw a houseboat with a charming upper deck, which included a grape arbor and lovely potted plants. A gorgeous little dark blue Porsche was parked at the quay.

The front steps of the bank at the top of rue du Conservatoire are often thronged with beautiful young men in pale pink shirts; French bankers are a miracle to behold. But the building deserves the description as well. Its stone is vermiculated, which means carved in shallow designs that look like the kinds of wiggling trails one sees in a child's ant farm. The effect is not beautiful close up, but from a distance, vermiculation gives the stone a kind of foggy beauty that eases its grandeur.

My great-uncle Claude writes that two "classes" of people come to Paris: those to whom the city will never be more than the sum of its parts, and those who grasp "the overpowering, constantly increasing sense of the great city's personality." To me, Paris feels like a jumbled-up buffet of earthly delights (lingerie and museums and cheese) — the "parts," that is — so I gather he would relegate me to that class. My betters (including Claude) discover Paris to be "delicately fanciful and gay," a persona grasped by those more discriminating sensibilities. Frankly, what I've read so far leads me to think that *Claude,* not Paris, was gay, notwithstanding the historical fact of his marriage, right there in black and white.

We found ourselves in a stretch of rue Saint-Denis that is the province of middle-aged sex workers, whores whom age has visited but not defeated. They were all accoutred appropriately, with high leather boots, bustiers, and tired eyes. They leaned against doorways on both sides of the street, at polite distances, and chatted desultorily while waiting for clientele who had not succumbed to a lust for youth.

Yesterday I bought warm gloves in aubergine. Last week I bought sleek shoes in the same color: lace-ups, with Italian toes. I feel like an answer to one of those fashion magazine questions: "Are you spring, summer, fall, or winter?" I guess I'm fall.

There is a bakery down the street from Anna's school, on avenue de Villars, where there is always a line. They specialize in little fruit tarts. The most beautiful one has figs sliced so thin as to be translucent, then dusted in sugar. Luca's favorite looks like a tiny version of the Alps: small strawberries, each one sitting upright and capped in a drop of white chocolate. My personal favorite has sliced apricots arranged in overlapping patterns, like crop circles in an English field.

Hôtel Drouot is the auction house where many Paris estates end up. You can stroll in and wander rooms filled with everything from fourteenth-century Flemish paintings and tarnished silver plate to groovy 1960s furniture. Today we rifled through boxes of old linens and army medals. I was particularly struck by a portrait of a boy and girl sitting in what seemed to be a 1970s living room. Where are those children now? Do they care that their rather sullen faces are being knocked down in an auction house — and finally sold only after an engraving of Japanese birds is added to the lot?

Anna and I were waiting on the Métro platform as a train arrived when I caught sight of a skinny, shaggy teen in a Keith Haring sweatshirt through the window. Luca! We managed to dash through the open doors just before they closed. There was my fifteen-year-old, chatting in Italian and looking too cool for words. "Honey!" I caroled out. I had forgotten one of life's cardinal rules. Teenage males do not care to be greeted by their mothers in front of peers. He turned his head and kept talking. Anna and I sat down.

I just discovered De Bouche à Oreille (By Word of Mouth), a store in the Marais with a trunk full of miniature globes about the size of your hand. There are ivory-colored, black (marked in white), or creamy blue-green. My impression is that you buy three or four and put them in a bowl, like fruit. They had a glass dome holding nothing but antique porcelain doll heads, antique compasses, and cool clocks embedded in glass balls, hanging from chains.

Alessandro thinks "our" homeless man is no drunk but a deaf-mute, since he hasn't said a word in the three months we've known him, if one can so label our relationship. We drop change in his hat, hand over cans of dog food, and pet the puppy, and he just smiles a truly sweet smile. To me he has an Eastern European face, rather round and stoic, as if his ancestors spent a lot of time picking potatoes in a chilly wind.

We have played good, supportive parents as Anna's teachers have yelled, stood her against the wall, and kicked her into the hallway. We have kept silent when the math teacher slapped a student with a book and made Domitilla shake in her boots. But today Anna came home in tears after the math teacher mocked her division (or her attempts at it). Alessandro is going in tomorrow, armed for bear. He's generally very calm, but when pressed, he pulls rank — as a professor and a member of the school board, not to mention a knight. That teacher had better Watch Out.

Anna and I had just entered the men's department of Galeries Lafayette to meet the male half of our family when Anna said, "Mama! Mama, look at them!" Automatically I began to reply, "Don't ever point . . ." when I saw where she was looking and my mouth fell open. Five men were strolling toward us wearing the smallest of tighty-nonwhities. Let me clarify that: five built, gorgeous, model-icious men, wearing only the briefest of briefs. They strolled along, chatting among themselves, advertising (I gather) their itsy-bitsy garments. The male shoppers didn't seem nearly as entertained as I was. In fact, although the men must have walked next to Alessandro, he claimed not to have noticed.

■ ■ ■ ■

Papa Bear (i.e., Alessandro) has returned triumphant from the Leonardo da Vinci School! Promises have been made about guarding Baby Bear's (i.e., Anna's) feelings. In return, Papa Bear has promised that said Baby Bear will stop chattering in class, will stop forgetting to bring her homework, and will forbear from announcing (this is a direct quote) "I didn't learn how to divide in my old school; they don't teach that in the States." 'Twas this last that invoked the math teacher's laughter (described by Anna as mockery), but really, one can hardly blame him.

GRIEF

In the grip of a vicious cold, I slunk back to bed after the kids went to school and buried myself in Kate Braestrup's memoir, *Here If You Need Me.* She is a chaplain attached to the search-and-rescue department of the Maine Forest Service, and her book starts when she suddenly finds herself a widow with four small children.

I started crying on cue, until a little further on in that chapter, when her seven-year-old son suggested that his father had already been reincarnated. As a tiger. At that, I laughed aloud, which turned into a pattern: moved to tears, soothed with laughter. Every once in a while I would glance out at the chilly, blue-gray Parisian sky, cuddle deeper into my down quilt, and pluck another tissue.

Alessandro came in to check on me at one point, sympathetic about my cold but very disapproving when he realized my pile of soggy tissues was the result of tears rather than a virus. "I never cry when I read," he pointed out, with perfect truth. His night-time reading, a biography of Catherine the Great, seemed unlikely to generate tears, even from one as susceptible to sentimentality as I. His book also didn't seem like much fun, especially after I inquired about the one thing I knew about Catherine — to wit, her purported erotic encounters with equines — and he informed me that the empress was a misunderstood feminist whose sexual inventory, while copious, was nevertheless conservative. Nothing to cry about there.

I shooed my husband out of the room and returned to my book and my Kleenex. Braestrup writes of a "hinge moment" — the second when you hear news that changes your life forever. I wept not just for her brave, funny state trooper of a husband, or for the child who drowned in an icy pool, or for the park ranger who curled his arms to demonstrate to Kate how he carried that child from the lake — but for the fear of that hinge moment in my own life, and the pure gratitude and relief of not having experienced it so far.

While reading, I silently reminded myself that Anna was too old to get lost in the woods, that I was never an outdoors type, that Alessandro hated picnics, that we never let our children out of our sight, and that I was too afraid of Lyme disease to go near a forest. About halfway through I made a mental note to stay away from the state of Maine altogether. Yet from the moment Braestrup describes her husband's fatal accident, she insists that no matter how *well* or how *carefully* or how *prudently* we love our children or our husbands or our dogs, there are no guarantees, and lives can be wrenched apart by death at any moment. When she writes of grief as a "splintery thing the size of a telephone pole" in your chest, her splinter endangers all the places of your heart.

Later, Alessandro brought me lunch: salad, a little steak, a chunk of Camembert, a clementine, a slice of almond cake for dessert. We ate in companionable silence, until he tried to wrest the book away. "What's the good of a book like that?" he wanted to know. "Now you'll dream about dead people." I do that anyway. Just a few nights before I had woken in the middle of a sentence that used *Mom* as punctuation. I stared into the dark for a while, trying to remember what she and I were talking about. Were we chatting about books? Was she sitting beside me, telling me something? Or was I only trying to get her attention, calling her name?

That's what Alessandro doesn't understand. A day spent crying in bed over stories of lost strangers gives you permission to cry for things over which you have no right to grieve: my children are alive and my mother died almost two years ago. Yet I wake thinking of her. I wish I could call her. I will always want her arms around me. I still want to cry for her.

My sister, Bridget, and her daughters are visiting. Jet lag triumphed and we didn't make it out of the apartment until six o'clock, when it was already dark and raining. We splashed along to the Centre Pompidou, the modern art museum. Anna and her cousins talked so intently about summer camp that they noticed they were in Paris only when a crepe stand came into view.

Milo has been back to the vet for a follow-up visit. To Marina's dismay, her Florentine vet labeled Milo obese, even after she protested that "he never eats." Apparently the vet's gaze rested thoughtfully on Milo's seal-like physique, and then he said, "He may be telling you that, but we can all see he's fibbing."

We went to a pharmacy to pick up some vitamin C, and Bridget, paying, confused fifty cents with fifty euros (and, it seems, vitamin C with gold dust); she offered the pharmacist three twenty-euro banknotes. The pharmacist's eyes widened: *"Ooooh, là là!"* he cried. I love moments when I feel as if I'm living in a French movie.

"Our" homeless man is not a deaf-mute, as Alessandro had conjectured. He spoke today, saying *"merci"* when Anna delivered a hopelessly ugly red squeaky toy for his puppy. Every day he sits to the side of the railing guarding the steps to the Métro, very bundled up and miserable-looking, with his dog in a cardboard box covered by a blanket, and a hat for money in front of the box.

I consider myself an academic before a romance writer, so I tend to particularly enjoy readers' letters pointing out errors — especially if the reader is wrong. Often I am castigated for using slang that readers are sure is modern but that is actually historically accurate. A favorite new example of this sort of word comes from Caleb Crain in *The New York Times Magazine;* he unearthed a letter from Keats, gleefully informing his brothers of the latest slang term for stopping at a tavern: "they call [it] 'hanging out.' "

Let me be the first to admit it: my Thanksgiving turkey was not all it could be. In fact, in flavor it brought to mind the Sahara desert. It was a strange turkey in the first place, as it came charred from having its feathers burned off, and wrapped in strips of lard. On the bright side, Bridget made fabulous gravy, and Alessandro's friend Donatella brought a mock pumpkin pie with a shiny orange top. It was in reality a custard tart with a glossy sheen: as if a pumpkin pie had been to Chanel and dressed for the occasion.

The homeless man is from Bucharest! Alessandro and Anna made conversation with him on the way to school today. He speaks very little French, so Alessandro is going to look up some phrases in Romanian. Apparently, the man said he wants to go home. I would, too. Paris is a chilly, hopeless place if you have nothing to do but sit and wait to be rained on.

In Notre-Dame: "How many people died

making this church?" Anna asked. And then, exasperated by my evasive answers ("lots . . . no, more than ten"), she stopped below the rose window. "Well, how many died making that? Don't you even know how many died putting it up there?" I discover, once again, that growing up is synonymous with disillusionment with one's parents.

I was fascinated in Notre-Dame by a priest, sitting at a businesslike desk behind a pane of bulletproof glass, offering confessions in either French or Arabic. He resembled nothing so much as a lower-level banker, the kind who should not be trusted to send an international wire.

It has apparently been cold and rainy in Florence for over a week, which is distressing to Marina. Milo is supposed to take a long walk every day to help him lose weight. But she never takes him outdoors when it rains, as she says he has a delicate constitution and doesn't digest well if he gets chilled. No one wants to know exactly how she has diagnosed this frailty.

Florent is back from Italy, and he and Alessandro met again. He is still in love with his beautiful Italian waitress, but he didn't manage to use any of the romantic phrases Alessandro taught him. He says he thinks she is interested, but he isn't quite sure, because of the language barrier. So he and Alessandro talked about the fact that Florent is buying land from a swindler who considers him easy prey because he is a foreigner. There is only one standing wall on Florent's land, but the Italian wants to sell the land as "with house."

Varenne Métro station is home to a huge replica of Rodin's *Thinker;* at some point a discourteous person knocked a roundish hole in his thigh, revealing that he is entirely hollow. This morning on the way to school Anna and I started discussing the family of mice who undoubtedly live inside. Anna suggested that Mama and Babbo would each sleep in one of the Thinker's big toes. I pointed out that Mama and Babbo like to sleep together, and she allowed that they could share one big one, while the babies had a small toe each.

The newest family game: pick on Mom by way of the pack of French language cards that everyone in the family knows except *moi.* Go on . . . ask me how to say *frog* in

French. I just learned it. My favorite card is *la girafe.*

Bridget and I took the girls off to Versailles, detouring at a photo booth in the Métro. Later Anna discovered to her horror that her beloved blue knit hat was gone, leading to tears and gnashing of teeth. On the way back, the children flew to the booth, but it was empty. Then my niece Nora shrieked. To the side sat a homeless person's blanket roll, the hat perched on top. But no home-less person. So . . . she stole it back!

The Hall of Mirrors at Versailles is gracious, elegant, and jaw-droppingly beautiful. I drifted down the center dreaming that I was a member of the *noblesse ancienne,* my imaginary skirts extending three feet to each side. We all had audio tours; over the elegant sound of a British man informing me about architectural details, I heard Anna talking to her cousin Zoe: "I dare you to pick your nose in front of that mirror. . . . Go on, I dare you!"

In Versailles, I bought a wonderful cook-book: *100 Recipes from the Time of Louis XIV.* Apparently, the court adored oysters and ate them along with both duck and leg of lamb. I am going to try chicken with champagne and the truly unusual cucumber fricassee. Almost every recipe calls for lard — and I can't imagine where one buys that in the United States.

This weekend we happened on a *brocante,* a string of small booths selling odds and ends, everything from chipped lamps to Elvis LPs. Our favorite table was selling twenty-two different kinds of homemade sausages. We bought five kinds, among which were wild boar and pepper-cured duck. Unfortunately I have no idea which is which, but last night I made a fabulous pasta sauce using wild boar or perhaps duck or, as Alessandro suggested, indigenous Parisian rat.

The homeless man has asked us to adopt his puppy as he wants to return to Bucharest and cannot take him. It's impossible, alas. We travel too much to own a dog that will soon be the size of an ottoman. Anna is devastated, and won't speak to either of us. Alessandro just found a friend who knows Romanian and got him to translate "Would you like us to make sure your dog is safe in a pet shelter?" This is not a popular option at home.

■ ■ ■ ■

We just took Luca's computer away for a month, after a very painful, blunt discussion with his Latin teacher (following painful, blunt discussions with his French and history teachers). They all said he was remarkably polite, which I'm proud about. But also remarkably indolent. Signed, Cruelest Parents in Paris.

We are now ensconced in the heart of a deeply conservative Catholic church — all "smells and bells," my mother would have described it. My favorite moment of the Mass is the final hymn, which is often a hymn to Mary, called "Couronnée d'Étoiles," or "Crowned with Stars." I love its wild purple prose. Every Sunday we less-than-tunefully carol that Mary "drapes" the sun, outshines the moon, and salutes the dawn.

Coming out of school, Anna told me that her gymnastics teacher has been asking "for a long time" that she bring a sweat suit, but "I kept forgetting." So we elbowed our way into a crowded department store, and she picked out a pink sweat suit with sequins

94

spelling FREE LOVE. "What's that mean?" she asked. I had no idea what to say, so I offered, "Love for lots of people, puppies and kittens, too." She nodded wisely.

My mother placed white sugar right next to crack cocaine in the catalog of the most dangerous substances known to man. To this day, my idea of heaven is a handful of small marshmallows: pure, undiluted, bad-for-you sugar in a form that could never be mistaken as healthy. I have found a supplier here in Paris, which is akin to a junkie discovering a private poppy field.

This morning as I watched Anna select pink undies, pink socks, and a pink shirt to go with her pink sweat suit, I grew suspicious and pried out the reason for this flare-up of conspicuous femininity: apparently she had been confronted in the bathroom by two malicious young ladies who said she looked like a boy and should use *their* bathroom. Because most people say Anna looks exactly like me, I find this particularly insulting (and absurd). But I sent her off to school looking like a sporty princess, armored in pink against her sharp-tongued foes, and then spent the morning brooding over it. Why are girls so mean to each other?

■ ■ ■ ■

Fridays are our date nights, which back in New Jersey meant movies, but here means food. Last night we wandered into one of the little covered passageways near us, the Passage des Panoramas. Inside, we found a bistro that could serve fifteen at most. The menu, on a chalkboard, offered a choice of precisely two entrées. I had smoky vegetable soup in a little tureen and then deep, delicious *boeuf bourguignon,* followed by warm chocolate cake. The cost was about fifteen euros. Joy!

"Our" homeless man is gone. Alessandro and Anna set off, our daily donation clutched in Anna's hand, only to find that he had vanished, presumably to Bucharest. Alessandro is berating himself for not trying out his phrase about dog shelters in time. I told a weeping Anna that the man couldn't bear to part from his puppy, so now that dog is learning Romanian. I hope this is the truth.

Today it hailed. The sky was actually the color of pearl, and when hail struck the roofs opposite my study, it bounced quite visibly. At the very top, the hail bounced from the ornate metal ridge that runs down the gable and formed little arches in the air, as if tiny fountains bloomed on the roofs.

This evening we ate at a sidewalk bistro. As twilight drew in, our waiter turned on a heat lamp. Across the street, a man played melancholy sax, leaning against the iron railings of the church. Winter is coming to Paris.

A Parisian Winter

The American media warn us at every turn that Christmas is a time of overindulgence. Women's magazines bulge with articles about how to avoid the buffet table, not to mention an extra ten pounds. But to be honest, that siren song of temptation has never bothered me much. English Department holiday parties tend to offer a dispiriting selection of cheap wine accompanied by three kinds of hummus. And I shed surplus calories by wrestling a five-foot tree into submission, grading my Shakespeare students' final papers, and fighting the lines to mail late presents.

My immunity was strengthened by my postcancer mood. Our kitchen used to be stacked with cookbooks and crockery, until I decided that it should be an ascetic feng shui retreat in which I would cook meals full of antioxidants. In one pot, because I gave all the rest away.

And then came December in Paris. Overnight our neighborhood covered market, Marché Saint-Quentin, was transformed into the movie set for a Dickens musical, complete with garlands and strings of lights. Our favorite *fromagerie* put out boxes of tiny quail eggs and three hitherto unfamiliar kinds of chèvre, produced only for the Christmas season. I was staggered by a mound of fresh mushrooms, big and ruffled like hats for elderly churchgoing fairies. It was only when the *marchand de fruits* asked me if I was quite sure I wanted that many that I realized this particular fungus cost the same as our rent.

Paris is always a materialist's playground, but December is in a class by itself. One day I wandered into the gourmet department of Galeries Lafayette to find that it had sprouted tables piled high with decorative flourishes for holiday baking: jars of edible gold leaf, silver stars, candied violets. The display was designed to tempt the unwary shopper not to gluttony per se — but rather to the pure beauty of food, to the ways it can be decorated and dusted and presented, turned into something that can take your breath away. I instantly succumbed to a wild desire for Staub minicocottes, enameled in a shiny burnt crimson. I bought eight of them, kissing the dream of an austere kitchen goodbye. Surely antioxidants taste better in cocottes.

But I didn't stop with cocottes. I bought a hand mixer that resembled nothing so much as a rather dangerous vibrator, rose-tinted Himalayan salt, and lavender-infused mustard in a moody violet color. It seems that Parisian ladies eschew leek soup in December, and spend their time crafting elaborate meals from ingredients few Americans have heard of. In short, I fell prey to the French version of holiday indulgence.

I made it home with aching arms, no gifts, and — more crucially — no bread. I was confronted with a grumpy Alessandro, who squinted at the Himalayan salt and demanded to know how I could possibly have forgotten to buy a baguette. By the time I came back from the *boulangerie,* Anna was chasing her brother through the apartment with my vibrating mixer. I ignored them and baked a chicken slathered in violet mustard. Honesty compels me to admit that the chicken was not a success. The children regarded it with the kind of expression with which a Californian greets a furry toilet seat cover. French children probably greet purple chicken with squeals of delight rather than demands that their parents hit the street for KFC.

Still, I began going to bed thinking about food. The remnants of a leg of lamb smeared with anchovies and butter could turn to a smoky broth, which then became fennel soup with spicy sausage (a recipe borrowed from Gordon Ramsay). I made the soup in a big pot. Then I put a few crispy sausage rounds in each cocotte, poured in some soup, and dripped spirals of spicy oil over the top. This felt a little like cheating: was I supposed to use my cocottes only to serve food baked therein? I felt sure that the Parisian answer would be a resounding yes. But then I remembered that when my parents were newly married and very poor, my mother served a group of unwary poets a silky meat pâté — made from cat food. My crimes pale in comparison.

I moved dreamily from one meal to the next. I used the cocottes to bake little chocolate cakes for a dinner party, mixing the very best chocolate — Michel Cluizel's — with splashes of Grand Marnier and a whole carton of eggs. Under the giddy influence of a Parisian December, I gave each cake a generous dab of crème fraîche and topped it with a translucent star made from pure spun sugar. The cakes looked gorgeous, but after my guests ate them up, their faces turned a bit green. Later I realized that the recipe promised a cake for ten, which I had poured into six pans.

Crème fraîche began entering the apartment in buckets, disappearing down the gullets of my family, my friends, and myself. In New Jersey, the children used to have pizza every Friday night and clamor to go to the Peppercorn diner for grilled American cheese on white bread. In Paris, they learned to smile at fennel soup and lick the spoon when they were finished.

Ascetism was relegated to the closet (unfortunately, so were my "thin" jeans). I finally discovered the allure of indulgence — along with a newfound appreciation for the luxury of time, born of being on sabbatical, free from committees, office hours, and classrooms full of students nervously waiting to be tested on *Hamlet.* I learned to think about food as being beautiful rather than just fattening or nourishing, as we Americans are too prone to doing. Throwing a cold pizza in the oven is easy; eating prepackaged sushi from the grocery store is even easier. Popcorn for supper so that one can work straight through the meal? Why not?

I am making only one New Year's resolution this year. I'm ignoring the obvious: my

102

overly tight clothing. Instead I will take my Parisian Christmas with me back to New York City in the fall. My cocottes will remind me that food is meant to be served to others, to be beautiful, to be original (even violet-colored), to be dreamed over. They will remind me that indulgence is not a virtue we should keep for the holiday season alone, and that saving time — when it comes to food — is more sinful than virtuous.

My Parisian December went a long way to mending a crack in my heart caused by the words "the biopsy was positive." To eat as the French do is to celebrate life, even to indulge in it.

Galeries Lafayette has put up its Christmas lights! The huge building has been transformed to a glowing set of rose windows that hark back to eighteenth-century Russia, or Versailles: a time when the display of beauty, its gleam and luxury, was of paramount importance. Of course, Alessandro pointed out that these windows beckon not to worship but to shop.

My favorite Galeries Lafayette holiday window is set with an exquisite dinner party scene: crystal chandeliers, fabulous dishes, tiaras scattered between the plates, wine glasses draped in pearls — all of it being enjoyed by assorted marionette bears. One has a wineglass in each paw and a tiara tipped over one ear. He raises the glasses drunkenly, toasting all the children outside the window.

The streets are suddenly filled with men selling chestnuts, roasted over oil barrels. Alessandro and I bought some, wrapped in twists of newspaper. They split open from the heat, showing sweet yellow insides. We walked along slowly, nursing the warm packages in our hands, eating smoky, slightly charred nuts.

Due to my disinclination to chop off chicken heads, my butcher whacks them off for me, but he leaves the knees: black and red, hard-scrabble knees for running hard. Parisian chickens are much more chickenlike than Mr. Perdue's; furthermore, eggs come ornamented with tiny feathers. My children shriek: "Butt feathers!" Having grown up on a farm, I like remembering the sultry warmth of newly laid eggs.

Anna and I were in a department store, weighing the merits of a stuffed penguin over a stuffed possum, when we were accosted by Santa Claus. This skinny, insistent Santa just wouldn't quit; he wanted a picture with Anna. Having been a micro-preemie, she's quite petite. But in her head she's a young lady of eleven, and young ladies do not sit on the laps of strange Santas. "You know what, Mama?" she said when he was finally banished. "That man was weird." And, a moment later, "I bet French Santas drink too much wine."

The rain comes down every day here; my umbrella is as crucial as my wallet. My favorite adaptation to the wet weather is babies in bright red backpacks that have four posts to hold little red canopies over their heads. They look like plump Indian rajas swaying along, atop paternal elephants.

Anna and I walked past yet another homeless man and his dog today. "He's a wiener dog!" said Anna. One look and I said, "No, *she's* a mama wiener dog." A wild scream followed. "Mama! She has puppies! Tiny puppies!" Sure enough . . . nine — *nine* — tiny, tiny puppies were inside the box on a warm grate. Two days old, according to their owner. We gave him all our change.

■ ■ ■ ■

We went with friends to the Champs-Élysées tonight for the first time since Christmas lights were put up. Trees all the way down the avenue are lit with tiny pale blue lights that slide downward, as if a lazy, bluish rain were falling.

Back in the States, we had a terrible time getting the kids up in time for church, often ending in most impious battles. Here we employ the mighty power of chocolate. I announce that if they rise immediately, we have time to go to a café for hot chocolate and croissants . . . then we walk through the chilly morning to a café and sit, fingers curled around big mugs of sweet chocolate, before we run to Saint-Eugène–Sainte-Cécile.

Our comfort food after a tough day at school is Japanese curry — specifically, Golden Curry made with five onions microwaved into pale, translucent, lettucelike pieces, as taught by my Japanese sister-in-law, Chiemi. The children gobble it the way a fat Frenchman gobbles foie gras: with concentration and delight.

■ ■ ■ ■

At fifteen, Luca has left "Mama" behind and now calls me "Mom," whereas Anna still howls "Mama!" across the whole apartment. It occurred to me yesterday that the day will come when no one will call me "Mama," and I won't realize it that day, or even the day after, just as I have no memory of Luca's last "Mama." There arc so many Last Times in parenting — the last book read aloud, the last nursing session, the last bath.

We have guests visiting from Florence, so parts of the family trekked to the top of Notre-Dame, about 380 steps. I stayed at ground level, tucked into a café, watching rain splash on chilled tourists. The children descended again very excited: on the very top of the cathedral the first snowflakes of the season had drifted into their hands, although down below there was nothing but rain.

A few days ago, Anna's Italian teacher burst into tears, which Anna credited to general class naughtiness. So today Domitilla showed up in a dress, according to Anna, and presented the teacher with a fancy notebook and three pencils "from the class" to make up for their misbehavior. Anna is very scornful of this effort.

Window shopping today at Nina Ricci: cream-colored silk pumps, with six-inch-high cork heels, from which pearls dangled. The shoes reminded me of a Christmas ornament I once made as a child, with stick pearls and a Styrofoam ball. A Kmart special for the very rich.

I have figured something out about living with a teenager: most conversations will not be successful, if that definition implies a meaningful exchange. If I snap, my fifteen-year-old son snarls back at me. If I'm in a good mood, I'll coax a sentence out . . . though if I ask what's happened at school, the answer is always: "Nothing." Leonardo da Vinci High School, otherwise known as the Black Hole of Paris.

Florent told Alessandro today that he is worried that his love for the Italian waitress will never come to anything. For one thing, he is forty-one and she is much younger, a university student when she is not waitressing. They did have a lovely evening together on his last visit. He talked most of the time, but she seemed responsive. I do not have a good feeling about this, but Alessandro says that romance writers should be more optimistic.

Street vendors are selling Christmas trees that are flocked white — but also bright scarlet and vivid purple. The department stores are piled with ornaments separated by color: here all black ornaments, there all transparent glass, or Pepto-Bismol pink. No one seems to offer life-size Santas entrapped in huge plastic fishbowls blowing with endless snow. Of course, there are no front yards, but I sense that's not the reason . . .

Last night Anna and her friend Nicole were building a complicated house in the living room, involving the couch, my yoga mat, a little table, a ton of blankets, et cetera. From my study, I could hear Nicole warbling on in her lovely English accent, then suddenly, "Anna, do I talk too much?" And, with the uncompromising honesty of childhood, the response: "Yes."

We went out for tea with Italian friends who professed themselves dazzled by the way Alessandro chatted with the waiter in

French. He smiled modestly . . . until the orders arrived. My cheese plate (*fromage* from the Gay Château) came as ordered, as did all other orders, except my husband's. He had requested a *tisane du berger* (a cup of tea), and a *lasagne aux aubergines* (eggplant lasagna) arrived instead. How the mighty have fallen!

Alessandro is making friends with the young, very conservative priest of Saint-Eugène–Sainte-Cécile. It turns out that our jewelry box of a church is famous for being the first church built of metal in all Paris. I can't see how this can be true: the walls are definitely made of stone. But one doesn't squabble with a priest over architectural details, not when there are so many more interesting things, like causes for the recent rash of pedophilia, that one can argue about. Our priest is mortified, and doesn't like to think about it.

Every night Anna and I lie in the dark for "talking time." I learned this from my friend Carrie, who defined talking time as a penalty-free half hour during which a child can confide secrets, such as whether she's being offered illegal substances. Anna talks of one thing: Domitilla. Today Domitilla was worse at math than Anna (inconceivable, frankly). . . . Domitilla's mother is nicer than I am, because Domitilla gets candy bars and chips for lunch. . . . Yesterday Domitilla wore a pink dress (withering scorn). No drugs, just pink dresses. Yawn.

Our local covered market is a visual feast. Arrangements of feathers — presumably donated by previous occupants — nestle decoratively among the plucked pheasants. Grapes hang from gnarled stands of grape wood, and fresh radishes are arranged in a shallow vertical box, greenery up the middle, red bulbs flashing like jewels along the sides. Today I ignored the pretty produce and, overcome by curiosity, brought home a black radish, a wrinkled and rather bendy phallic horror. Investigating it on the Internet, I discover that flaccidity is no better in a radish than it is (ahem) in a man.

A huge Ferris wheel, the kind with glassed-in, heated compartments, has been erected at one end of the Champs-Élysées. The children have taken several rides, so now only one thing really interests them: the VIP car, which has smoked glass to protect its Very Important People. Anna is convinced that, if she's lucky, one day she'll see Malia and Sasha Obama spinning above Paris.

As winter tightens its grip, it feels as though we emerge into a slightly darker street every morning. Peering into lighted windows of hotels on our walk to the Métro, we see fewer breakfast guests every week.

My French friend Sylvie and I went to a wonderful little museum today, the Musée Nissim de Camondo. Moïse de Camondo was a fantastically wealthy Jewish banker and a collector of art and eighteenth-century furniture. In 1911 he had a mansion built to house his collections, basing its design on that of the Petit Trianon at Versailles. He snapped up furniture when great estates were dissolved, even buying paneling from the apartment of the Count de Menou, and then lived there for years in the midst of truly royal splendor. I find his obsession fascinating and sad; he could certainly decorate his rooms with Queen Marie Antoinette's vases and re-create the atmosphere of eighteenth-century nobility — but as a Jew and a banker, he could never have been part of it.

Today I passed an open-faced workshop, in the front of which a man was shaping metal with a saw. Bright orange sparks spun from his saw, flying in a high arc to land on the jeans of the man behind him, on two chairs, and on another workbench. They seemed like bright snow, unthreatening, disappearing on contact.

Today Domitilla got a *"bravissima"* in Italian grammar and Anna got only a *"brava."* So Anna promptly burst into tears. The poor teacher, who likely had no idea of the various tensions in the room, gave a speech about how wonderful Anna is, which my ungrateful daughter declared to be boring and embarrassing.

We bought a Christmas tree yesterday. In Paris they are sold with trunks whittled to points and jammed into stands made from logs. I approve, as this obviates the annual blasphemy provoked by complicated tree stands. But I also disapprove, because without water, how long will this tree keep its needles? Still, it has very kindly given the living room its elusive smell of the deep forest.

Anna suffered through two years of unrequited love at ages eight and nine, and she's rather proud to be fancy-free here in Paris.

A boy from her class followed us through the turnstile at the Métro today and darted over to ruffle Anna's hair before running away. "That boy has a crush on you," I observed, stating the obvious. "Four of them do," she said with total indifference.

A few days ago, the pen pal Alessandro had when he was just a boy, between 1974 and 1984, sent him an email out of the blue. After much exclaiming, they Facebook "friended" each other, and Andrzej, who's from Poland, got around to investigating the pictures on Alessandro's Facebook page. He wrote back today to say that *his wife is an Eloisa James reader!* She's a Polish banker, and presumably has been reading the Polish translations.

Today Paris is bitterly cold — below freezing. I bundled up and walked to a department store to buy Christmas presents. As I approached the shining windows, I realized that a woman was seated on a doorstep with a simple sign, J'AI FAIM or "I'm hungry." Clutched in her arms was a five-or six-year-old child, his head on his mother's shoulder. Paris is by turns the most beautiful city in which I've lived — and the most heartbreaking.

114

■ ■ ■ ■

Anna's elementary school gave their Christmas concert today, so Alessandro and I trudged through the snow to see it. Last night Anna revealed that she knew only the first line of every carol in Italian; after that she planned to switch to English. To all appearances, no one noticed. My favorite moment was when the entire school sang, in thick Italian accents, "Last Chreeestmas, I gave you my 'eart . . ."

It's snowing again and the roofs opposite my study window have turned white. The sky is precisely the same milky color, so where the black, notched roof ridge meets the sky, it looks like a black railway track stretching across some vast and snowy Russian landscape.

Returning from Christmas shopping yesterday, Alessandro announced, "I bought myself some sweaters, you'll like them, they're not all the same." Parisian men wear thick crimson pullovers and plum-colored boots. I opened the shopping bag to find that Alessandro had bought four sweaters. Three were black. One distinguished itself by being gray with black stripes.

I am in a fit of domestic fervor directly linked to my mother-in-law's imminent arrival; Marina could take down Bobby Flay without blinking an eye. My goal is to serve only homemade broths — not that she'll be particularly impressed, since she wouldn't imagine another option.

I have discovered the French equivalent to a dollar store. I bought a plum-colored colander for seven euros, Christmas ornaments that look like miniature 1960s "mod" lamps for two euros each, and, for four euros, a fabulous lime green mold for making little cakes. My favorite purchase was Christmas tree lights, each enclosed in an ornate metal ball. Alessandro tells me they are classic, identical to lights from his childhood.

In Church with Scrooge

Having no particular knowledge of the minutiae of the liturgical calendar, it was pleasant to discover one Sunday in December that there was a special celebration going on for *les enfants;* accordingly, more babies and small children than usual were in attendance. In the chair next to us sat a plump and very happy boy who was just learning to walk. He and Anna had such a good time handing a toy cellphone back and forth that he kept spitting out his pacifier and crowing with joy.

The cheerful priest began his homily and then kept going, and going. The baby kept crowing, and crowing. The toy phone hit the stone floor a few times.

Then, from a row at the front of the nave, there rose a gaunt and ancient man, dressed completely in black, including the overcoat that swung behind him. He turned around and walked, scowling, straight toward us.

The entire congregation froze, watching as this Scrooge-like menace advanced. The priest's eyes widened visibly. Monsieur le Scrooge turned along the side aisle, now obviously coming to confront the baby's *maman.*

Heads swiveled in unison to follow his progress. The child's mother swept him up against her shoulder in a gesture that reminded me of the protective moves made by mothers in films when towns are invaded by Nazis, or aliens. "Madame!" we heard M. Scrooge say in a gravelly, outraged voice, but she was already fleeing to the back of the church, abandoning the toy cellphone on the floor.

Mission accomplished, Scrooge turned back toward his seat. The priest and parishioners watched him scowl his way up the aisle. Once it was safe, Anna trotted after the mother, waving the toy phone. For a moment I thought our sweet, curly-haired priest would say something about this small drama; it was, after all, a Sunday for *les enfants.*

But instead there was silence as he blessed the Host, and then from the other side of the nave, far behind us, came a defiant series of squawks. The baby and his *maman* were undefeated!

When it came time to go forward for Holy Communion, Scrooge rose to his feet before the priest had finished speaking, securing himself a place at the very front of the line. Upon receiving Communion, rather than return to his seat, he planted himself next to the priest's elbow and turned as if to adore the altar.

"He's going to accost her when she takes the Host!" Alessandro said, with obvious and impious delight. But no, it was not to be: the young mother took the Host without incident. M. Scrooge's plan — whatever it was — was foiled by an elderly woman in a wheelchair who forced him to move to the side.

The young priest, making the best of a bad situation, put his hand on the child's round head, blessing him and, presumably, all his squawks and squeaks.

Today Alessandro and Anna flew off to snowy Florence, where they're turning around after a couple of days and driving back to Paris with elderly Italian family members and one obese Chihuahua in tow. I wish it would stop snowing as I'm afraid the car will crash while crossing the mountains. The memoirist Elizabeth Stone wrote that having children is like letting your heart walk around outside your body, and mine is going to be crossing the Alps.

I bought some presents at Galeries Lafayette this afternoon, a soft heather-colored scarf and a lacy shirt for my college roommates. Dusk was gathering as I left the store. Just outside on the snowy street, a stand was brewing soup in cast-iron pots, so I bought a cup of lentil soup with Indian spices and walked home, the soup warm in my hands, exploding on my tongue.

Yesterday Luca and I were roaming in the twilight when we passed a tiny bar with scarlet walls and a deep couch. A man inside leaned forward to smoke an ornate silver hookah. I delightedly informed Luca that it must be an opium den, rattling on about the Victorians and their more louche habits, before I remembered to add a little lecture on the perils of drugs. Unfortunately for my exotic tourist moment, Wikipedia suggests that the man was smoking tobacco in a "Hookah Lounge."

I have decided to use my beloved cocottes to create individual drunken-cherry cakes for Christmas dinner. Venturing out to buy the cherries, I survived the crowds by pretending I was a fish caught in the Gulf Stream. There is no point in fighting the current, no need to use fins; just gently bump the others in your school as you swim, and remind yourself that breathing is unnecessary because you're a fish.

In the interest of empirical research, I have been gathering family gossip about Great-Uncle Claude. It's reported that he had a "tempestuous" relationship with Ivé, who finally left him for a German man. Because — and this is a direct quote from one of my uncles — "he was not up to her sexual energy." I knew it! Apparently my great-aunt Genevieve, a terrifying woman who used to stamp about in a long cape, wrote her brother a letter telling him to "act like a man" and stop being pushed around by Ivé. To no avail, one assumes.

Today I tried a traditional French delicacy called *andouillette,* which is a sausage made from a pig's intestine (chitterlings). I'm determined to investigate all the food that I reflexively avoided as a younger person, but I shall continue to avoid this one. Once cut, the sausage fell into pieces whose original design was all too evident. In short, the texture was revolting. Culinary adventurousness can go only so far.

Yesterday I realized that a rental apartment implies a naked Christmas table. So I ventured into a chic store and bought black glass votive cylinders with a black-on-black velvet fleur-de-lis pattern. Once home I realized that they were designed by someone with plans for enjoying an exciting evening of illegal substances, not singing "Silent Night." I have shopping remorse, which is presumably not as bad as tattoo remorse, but still stinging.

After being delayed by snow, Anna, Alessandro, and Italian family members arrived last night at 10:30. Anna tore through the house, wild with excitement when she saw the tree and presents. "Don't look!" I shouted. She had told me on the phone from Italy that she now liked Barbies. I was surprised because she had never shown interest before, but after surveying forty dolls, I picked one and some extra shoes, since I have always admired Barbie's shoe collection.

On his first night in Paris, it looked as though Milo was planning to sleep on Luca's bed (he used to be Luca's dog). But to

Luca's dismay, at the last minute Milo waddled off to sleep on his red velvet cushion, on the floor next to Marina's bed.

The following note — reproduced here without correction — was hand-delivered by Anna in the morning before breakfast: "Dear Mama, I don't like barbies. That's why before you tould me to, I looked at and shook a present from you and dad. And I'm REEALLY SORRY! PLEASE FOGIVE ME!"

Today Marina announced that she wants to buy Milo a raincoat as a Christmas present. So the family — sans Milo — trooped out to a shop in the Marais that sells accoutrements for small dogs. Anna snatched up a tiny, blossom pink confection trimmed with rhinestones (I might add that Milo is aggressively male, and fond of attacking dogs four times his size). Flouting the girlie stereotype, Alessandro inquired if the coat came in a larger size. The shopkeeper asked about Milo's breed, in order to choose the appropriate coat size. "No, no, he's not Chihuahua-size," Alessandro told him. "He's more like bulldog-size." The shopkeeper looked most disapproving, and pointed toward three or four coats in the corner: the plus-size department. From these meager pickings, we chose a transparent raincoat with jaunty purple trim.

It's December 23 and I feel glum. I don't want the Christmas season to end, because it's the only time I can legitimately indulge one particular addiction: glitter. When else can you pull out fourteen bottles of shining sand, glitter shaped like stars, glitter glue? Only in December does the floor around the kitchen table sparkle in the sunlight and a child's hair gleam — no, glitter — as if fairy dust were caught in the strands.

On Christmas Day I cooked twice: first, a huge goose that had been blanched and air-dried for two days, stuffed, and presented in shallot Madeira sauce; then, in the late evening, a very simple risotto, the kind I can make blindfolded. The goose lost to the risotto, hands down, even though its crispy skin was perfectly set off by the Madeira sauce, which balanced the touch of wildness lent by the bird. One of the hardest things for me to remember is that just because a dish takes six hours in the kitchen it will not necessarily make guests as happy as a familiar recipe done well.

■ ■ ■ ■

I have decided to single out a few moments from this Christmas and try, mindfully, to preserve the memories. So here's one: in a kitchen fragrant with the smell of roasting goose, Alessandro discovered me alone and grabbed the chance for a kiss and an enthusiastic grope.

An important part of preserving memories is deliberately letting some go. Careful editing, if you will. I plan to forget the moment when my sister-in-law surveyed the Christmas table and said, "Did you forget that I don't eat meat?" (This, after eating copious amounts of prosciutto at lunch.) Ditto when she picked up her plate and dumped her sweet potato puree on her mother's plate, saying, "I usually like puree, but this one . . . no."

This morning we went to Mass at Notre-Dame Cathedral, which included two bishops, more incense than a hippie party, and glorious choral music. I confiscated Anna's Skipper doll (you know, Barbie's younger sister) at some point, and realized only after taking Communion that Skipper's pink-

and-blond head was sticking out of my bag and bobbing down the aisle with me.

Even though Alessandro bought himself three black sweaters just before Christmas, my present — a black sweater — was quite successful. My husband employed precisely the same guidelines as I had when choosing his gift: he bought me a huge, gorgeously heavy, Staub pot. He chose black.

We are all rather horrified to find that the transparent raincoat, designed for a French bulldog, does not fit around Milo's ample middle. It doesn't have a prayer of fastening. Marina has been forced to concede that perhaps Milo should go back on his diet. We keep pointing out the svelte, lively dogs who trot by us on morning walks: it seems that neither French women nor their dogs get fat.

We have discovered an enchanting bead and jewelry-making supply store, Tout à Loisirs, in the Marais. It's designed as a series of alcoves; to the left, every alcove is distinguished by color. I fell in love with Venetian blue glass beads ornamented with twirly black lines. To the right, the alcoves represent different countries: for example, Indian beads of every shape and size, including shiny pendants of laughing Hindu deities. We bought tiny butterflies with translucent wings, flowers cut from super-thin metal, and cameos with eighteenth-century heads.

I am fraying under the pressure of cooking two meals a day for the extended family, so last night my own family joined me in the kitchen. I made risotto (now a nightly request from the Italian contingent); Anna chopped; Alessandro washed and — ta-da! — Luca looked up how to cook a pork chop on Google and then created succulent breaded pork chops. At dinner, we all lauded him and then talked of other things. Twenty minutes later he said, "Let's talk more about my chops! Lavish me with praise!" Welcome to the world of thankless domestic labor, sweetie.

Paris presents structural difficulties for the disabled, such as narrow sidewalks and cobblestones. Yet those unavoidable difficulties are ameliorated by kindness: when we pushed my sister-in-law's wheelchair to the door of Notre-Dame, we were whisked past the line of people waiting to enter the cathedral and seated just below the altar. Coming into a department store cafeteria full of people trolling constricted aisles for seats, we were instantly ushered to an available table. Waiters in an outdoor café on the Champs-Élysées pulled apart and reconfigured elaborate rows of seats to accommodate her chair.

The arched roof of Marché Saint-Quentin is made of glass, and yesterday evening we realized that its strings of blue and white Christmas lights reflect against the dark night sky, as if the heavens had revealed themselves to hold busy highways running with stars. Anna amended my description: the heavens hold *fizzy,* starry highways.

I cooked duck breasts for dinner, first marinating them in red wine and garlic, and then pan-searing them with a pear and Grand Marnier sauce. Afterward Luca, who pours ketchup on everything from French fries to escargots, waved his unopened ketchup bottle in the air and announced: "Do you know what this means, Mom?" Yes, I do. It means that somewhere, in some remote part of the world, a pig just levitated gracefully and flew around his pen, that's what.

A row of elegantly narrow dormer windows

sprouts from the building opposite my study. Sometimes a gaunt woman with beautiful cheekbones and sleek black hair pushes open her window and leans out, smoking and flicking the ashes onto the slate. Today she wears a red dress and looks as if she belongs in an eighteenth-century novel, the kind in which heroines come to a bad end.

It was New Year's Eve last night, so the family drank champagne and ate oysters on the half shell. Alessandro's mother tolerated the champagne, although she said the Italian version, prosecco, is better for one's digestion. The oysters had been harvested that morning, and still had the faintest tang of the sea, like the memory of a briny swim in childhood. At midnight the Eiffel Tower burst into a shower of sparks, and 2010 slipped in the door.

At one end of our street is an excellent kosher restaurant, Les Ailes. The first time we ate lunch there, in the fall, we were fascinated by a middle-aged couple, who we quickly decided were lovers married to other people. They leaned close, eating with an air of heat and excitement. Over time, and subsequent lunches, we have concluded that Les Ailes is a playground for adulterous frolics; we can always find a couple in the room who qualify. But yesterday, escaping from our houseful of relatives, I realized that Alessandro and I probably looked like adulterous lovers, giddy with freedom and delighted by food we hadn't cooked.

In France the Boy and Girl Scouts are organized by parish. This morning both troops sat just in front of us in church, wearing little berets with blue crosses and long shorts, although the winter air has a snap to it. Our neighborhood is very multicultural, but these scouts looked like a French advertisement from the 1940s: Caucasian, neatly kempt and behaved, wearing their red scarves and berets with unconscious but distinct flair. The retro vibe of these homogeneous scouts is not entirely attractive.

After careful inspection, Marina decided this morning that Milo has gained weight since arriving in Paris. This caused a crisis, exacerbated when Anna confessed that Milo had just snatched and eaten a chocolate cellphone. Contrary to everything we had heard about chocolate's toxicity to dogs, Milo remains hale and hearty, not to mention hungry. He has indeed gained a Parisian pound and will be allowed no more holiday prosciutto.

In the window of Emanuel Ungaro, a mannequin stands with her back to us, gesturing toward an invisible companion. She wears reckless hot pink, a long swath of silk that leaves most of her back bare. Rather than overtly selling the gown, the display subtly reminds us that we stand in the dark with chilly noses and snowy feet, and somewhere . . . where *she* lives . . . the very air breathes luxury.

Anna in the bath, arguing over her bedtime. "Why," she wants to know, "can Luca stay up until ten o'clock and I can't?" "Because he's fifteen," say I, "and when he was eleven, he had to go to bed at eight o'clock, too." "How do you know?" she demands. "Because I'm the mother of both of you!" "You might not be," she points out. "You might be only a mother in disguise."

Paris is so cold that I keep going into the kitchen and opening up the little furnace, as much to encourage the poor creature as to warm my hands. On the Métro this morning, I noticed that women are adapting by adding an extra scarf. One woman wore silk embroidered in small flowers next to her face, and a ruby cable-knit scarf, almost a shawl, wrapped around her shoulders.

Anna owns a hotly prized possession: a tiny pink eraser in the shape of a hamster, given to her by cousins in Michigan. "So you see," Anna explained, "everyone loves it because Paris doesn't have anything like *this*." Oh, those deprived Parisians. Apparently of all the kids, Domitilla loves it most. "She said, 'I love it, I love it, I adore it, please can I play with it?' " Anna reported. *"And?"* I prompted, hopefully. Anna gave me a scornful look.

Last night we had a dinner party and invited Alessandro's conversation partner Florent, so I finally got to meet him. He is absolutely lovely — tall, lean, very handsome, and very, very French. He has brown hair and beautiful green eyes. What's more, he teaches language and literature to middle school students and actually *likes* adolescents. I think he is perfect and could match him with any number of single friends at home. But Alessandro says that his heart belongs to the Italian waitress.

Given my New Year's resolution, which was

to acquire a Parisian level of elegance pretty darn quick, I thought it behooved me to go shopping. Today is the start of biannual sales in shops throughout Paris. The French government allows only two sale events a year, regulating markdowns in department stores as well as in, for example, the fashionable (and expensive) shops on rue du Faubourg-Saint-Honoré. Have you seen the Filene's Basement wedding-dress event on television? Add the security guards from Walmart's "Black Friday" sales, keeping back the hordes so that innocent salespeople aren't literally trampled to death. I aged five years in Galeries Lafayette, so I'm not sure my new black boots will get much use.

On the way to the Marché Saint-Quentin, we pass a small shop with crates of different oyster varieties arranged in the window. Three gnarled gentlemen stand behind a counter; they wear heavy gloves and crack open oysters. It takes surprising physical strength: they wrench the wrinkled, defensive shells open and flip them onto platters, joking among themselves the whole time.

We must return the chic little raincoat that cannot be fastened around Milo's rotund middle, but meanwhile Anna has been playing with it. She has it bunched over her head and belted under her chin. She says it's a welding helmet and that she's "Anna, Secret Agent Man." I asked her what the Secret Agent Man was doing, and she said she was "seeking out the awesomeness": that is to say, trying to break into Luca's bedroom, strictly off-limits to younger sisters.

For Christmas, my stepmother sent Anna a gorgeous hat: hand-knitted in Minnesota, of nubbly purple wool trimmed with wooden beads. On top is a small tassel with a bead at the end. It's an adorable creation that reminds me of hats worn by Norwegian elves in children's picture books. I find it very moving, and a bit homesick-making, to look down in a crowded Métro station and see this scrap of Minnesota handiwork bobbing its way through Paris.

We took Milo with us to the fancy dog apparel store in order to guarantee a coat that fit. Alas, we had to take an aesthetic step down from purple trim: the sole coat that fits our obese dog is camouflage green, seemingly designed for a dog being kitted out for a paramilitary operation. Marina was greatly taken by bright pink dog booties. Milo doesn't care for his new jacket, and I hate to think about his reaction to those boots.

Luca has started twice-a-week night classes in French. Because he is bilingual, he has a beautiful accent, but he is still far behind the rest of the ninth-grade class, most of whom have at least one French parent. "What are the other students like?" we asked at dinner. "Older," he said, with a mischievous grin, and then refused to say anything other than to observe that their lives were more interesting than his.

Yesterday I ventured back into the Great Sales. I found myself in a dressing room next to a teenager cheerfully driving her mother crazy by trying on sexy clothing. *"Oh, là là!"* Maman cried; from her description the skirt was as high as her daughter's armpit. The next outfit wasn't much better. *"Oh, là là!"* Maman exclaimed. *"Oooh, là là!"* For my teenager's part, Luca slouched off to school today with hair like a toilet brush; it's so nice to know that teenagers are the same the world over. *OOOH, LÀ LÀ,* indeed.

The huge lingerie department at Le Bon Marché was crowded with tables of markdowns, women ruffling through them as

135

intently as if they were looking in a box of old photographs for their first love. I discovered that French women wear undies of pink pleated satin, fanciful white lace, and translucent pearly silk, but they don't wear cotton. I left empty-handed, unable to give up my Jockeys for Her for these delectable hand-wash-only confections. Still, I find myself thinking about the bras . . . perhaps it is time to turn my back on cotton.

Paris is triggering one of the friction points in my marriage. Our apartment was built in the 1700s, and the windows are original. *Brrr.* Alessandro turns the heat down; I hike it back up. He says the heating bill will impoverish us, but I insist on being warm. We have been having this battle for sixteen years. Hopefully, we will have it for many years to come.

Milo is a dog with an undiscriminating palate; today he shredded — and then ingested — a plastic baby bottle belonging to a purring stuffed bear. Anna has been flinging herself around the apartment, melodramatically announcing that now her baby will *staaarve.*

Luca told me he didn't want to do his

homework "because there is no point because in 2012 we will all be blown into
dust," and he will have wasted his time in
school. I asked where he learned this crucial
and terrifying information, and he admitted
"crazy people on the Web. But," he added,
"crazy people are often right." Cruelly, I
continue to ruin his brief time on earth by
insisting he study the Romans.

Yesterday our priest's solo singing during
the Mass wavered up and down; a bit later
he suddenly dropped a sentence about the
importance of baptism, said he felt ill, and
walked out. In the United States, the congregation would have instantly started chattering to each other. But the French are utterly composed; the whole church waited
silently, and five minutes later another priest
dashed in, announced that all was well, and
smoothly took up the sermon on baptism.

VERTIGO

This morning the snow was coming down fast in rue du Conservatoire, slanting sideways and turning the gray slate roofs the color of milk. I leaned against my study window, idly thinking about how passionately children love snow, when I realized that I was peering down at a group of Parisian women in the street below, engaged in the rapid-fire kissing of a wintry hello. Growing up on the farm, we'd braved snowstorms in puffy coats (preferably lurid orange, the better to avoid being targeted by a hunter who'd killed a six-pack rather than an animal); these women wore dark coats belted tightly around their slim waists. As they bent toward each other, pecking like manic sparrows, their scarves flashed magenta, lavender, dull gold. From my vantage point, far above them, they looked like inhabitants of a different world, as dissimilar to me as a gaggle of peacocks to a turkey.

One year, when we had even less money than usual, my mother took down the dining room curtains, which were printed with fifteenth-century sailing ships, and made back-to-school dresses for my sister and me. Even though the politically correct contingent wouldn't turn Christopher Columbus from saint to devil for another twenty years, I was an early adherent of the Loathe-the-Conquistador club, thanks to being forced to wear the *Niña,* the *Pinta,* and the *Santa María* all that year, snow or shine.

The Parisiennes in my street had never worn dining room curtains. You could just tell. The moment I allowed that certainty to sink into my mind, unfortunate scenes from my high school years lit up in my memory like a horrible TV show from the seventies. My prom party was held in a gravel pit, though I don't remember the party nearly as vividly as I do the dress I wore — sadly, I find this to be true of many occasions. I had earned the money for it waitressing at DeToy's Supper Club. The manager made us wear polyester dirndl skirts and white blouses that pulled down over our shoulders; we looked like von Trapp wannabes. I took my waitressing money and bought a

139

prom dress in the precise shade of pink that would most clash with my hair. My date brought me a bouquet of nearly dead roses. I had to cradle them in the crook of my elbow, but their heads kept slipping off my arm like a drunken woman being carried to bed.

Over the years I've tried to explain to Alessandro what growing up on a farm in the upper Midwest, outside a town of 2,242 people, was like. He's never quite been able to grasp it. He grew up in Florence, Italy, and his experience in, and with, America is largely limited to the East Coast. Furthermore, he has an annoying way of trying to top my stories. If I describe the trauma of circling the gym in a salmon-colored dress to the dulcet strains of "Stairway to Heaven," he'll counter with a tale about a family trip to Switzerland.

Thus, when I received an invitation to my twenty-five-year high school reunion a few years ago, it seemed the perfect moment to introduce him to my past. We arrived in Madison to find that its population had shrunk by more than half. There was one pickup truck halfway up Main Street and — I kid you not — a tumbleweed rolling toward us. I peered at Alessandro to make sure he registered the symbolism, but his face was lit up, reveling in the possibility that gunslingers might leap out from behind the Shear Salon, à la spaghetti westerns that he'd grown up with.

The reunion itself was held in the VFW lounge, which was in a basement. I told myself that it was all going to be different. I was a *professor* now, not to mention a *New York Times* bestselling writer. I could hold my head high; my failure to make the cheerleading team was far behind me. But alas: the painful glaze of humiliation that plagued me in high school rushed back the moment I saw the same clusters of people, still talking together, two and a half decades later. Though, of course, the subjects of those conversations had changed. "She fired that shotgun right through the ceiling," one of my classmates whispered. "She was hoping to hit that worthless husband of hers — he was carrying on an affair right in her bed — but instead she shot the sheriff. Got him right in the foot." I was opening my mouth to ask what the sheriff was doing in the assailant's bedroom, but she had already moved on. "You did hear about Lindsey-Ray, didn't you?" I shook my head. "She moved in with seven or eight gay men down in Minneapolis," she said, "and then got pregnant. Kind of a miracle birth, doncha think?" The drinks had turned out to be vodka with a splash of juice, and Alessandro grew very cheerful, periodically circling back to me to report on his conversations like a slightly drunk Garrison Keillor. "Did you talk to that woman who already has six grandchildren? Amazing!" He shook his head in disbelief. We had barely recovered from toilet training, so he hadn't noticed that procreation can start early.

After what felt like yet another four-year ordeal, the evening's program got under way. A class member who now happened to be the mayor of Madison started awarding prizes. I honestly can't remember why I won a prize; as with the prom, a sartorial detail eclipsed the main event. When I walked to the front of the room, I was presented with a huge, dingy pair of men's boxer shorts, stapled to two slats of wood, with a rope slung on the top. A "Norwegian handbag," the mayor called it. I carried this object back to our table, trying to smile like a good sport.

Finally, finally, *finally,* I saw on Alessandro's face the expression that should have been there all along: pure horror. "Did they give that to you because you write romance?" he whispered. I had no idea. In fact, I can't even remember what came next.

Maybe the whole room went home with Norwegian handbags; maybe the reunion committee had stayed up all night staple-gunning their grandfathers' undershorts to bits of wood. Back in the day, I had known instinctively that I was never going to fit in — and I'd blamed my mother and those dining-room-curtain frocks. But in light of my Norwegian handbag, I am inclined to forgive her.

She wanted us to be ladies, to leave Madison, and to raise our children in a place where no one had heard of a Norwegian handbag. These days, I own a magenta scarf and high-heeled black boots. I live on the other side of the ocean from Minnesota. I survived the year of wearing the dining room curtain, and lived to tell the tale.

The women below my study window had stopped pecking at each other and had gone their separate ways. And the snow was still falling, in that directed, intense way that snow falls in Minnesota and, apparently, in Paris as well.

Too much chocolate and crusty bread. . . . I have determined that I should walk up the stairs to our apartment on the fourth floor once a day. With only one apartment per floor, this sort of invasion is new to the little dog who lives below us. He starts growling when my foot touches the first stair; he's barking by the second level; he's a lunatic by the third. As I open my door, I'm panting heavily, and I imagine that he is too, exhausted by the demented Paul Revere act that no one hears but the two of us.

Snow on the dark gray tiles opposite my study window looks like white fur clinging to the roof, as if the house were growing a protective coat against the freezing air. But I am learning Paris now: by afternoon a chilly sun will emerge. The snow-fur will molt, and water will rush into drains under the street.

Putting away groceries as I snapped out domestic commands, I dislodged the ice tray, and ice cubes skittered all over the floor. Alessandro bent to pick them up, but a glitch in the space-time continuum intervened and he was thrown back to age nine. I found myself trying to fight off an impudent boy sticking ice down my neck.

This morning I walked down rue de Cléry, where little storefronts hold nothing but rolls of fabric, built into log-cabin-type castles. As I walked on, the stores grew more stylish, and the fabric changed from bright polyesters to creamy linens and exquisite silks. No longer piled up like logs, these rolls stand on their ends, a drape of upholstery fabric pulled to the side to display fiery red flowers, next to a roll of dusky heather tweed fit for a Scottish lord striding the moors.

On the shabbier end of rue de Cléry: a lace shop with thousands of samples spilling from cabinets lining its narrow walls. Close to the door are laces in persimmon and saffron, embedded with tiny mirrors. Stuffed alongside are spools of black lace sewn with teardrop pearls, copper ruffles, and (presumably) fake ermine trim, garish but gay.

A full renovation has begun in the apartment above us. In the kitchen we have what's called in the trade a "coolie lampshade," shaped like a very broad cone. We've just discovered water flowing steadily down the cord and the shade, organizing itself into drops around the edge of the shade, then falling in straight lines like tinsel. Alessandro ran upstairs and returned with the head workman. He walked into the kitchen, took stock of the situation, and said, "Don't use that light — it might not work."

Can there be a crueler fate than the need to diet in Paris? I'm not saying that I regret all that crème fraîche, because I don't. But unless I buy a whole new wardrobe, I must exercise restraint. I gather French women drink a lot of leek soup (not the creamy kind) when they have to reduce. I simply write down everything I eat. In short: I thin by shame, rather than by leek broth.

The sky is a cloudless bright blue, and yet somehow little snowflakes are drifting down outside my window. They float sideways, looking fluffy and indecisive, as if they belong in another part of the world and are falling here by accident.

Anna revealed, five minutes before bedtime, that last week her music teacher had yelled at her until she promised to practice her recorder. "But I forgot," she said, shrugging. "Now he's going to yell at me again." "Where's the recorder?" I demanded. "You can practice right now!" *"Mammma,"* she said with a roll of her eyes, "it's in my boot, at school, where it always is. If I brought it home, I might lose it." Such impeccable logic.

■ ■ ■ ■

My excuse for why my French is terrible is that my head is filled with English words. I like to think about their nuances. Take *gay,* for example. It's a shame it's all but lost its original meaning; to me, it has a kind of tinsel joy, like waltzing on the deck of the *QE2,* or the feeling of swing music, played at a frantic beat and danced to by soldiers returning to the front.

Milo still loves Luca — his original owner — dearly, though it has become manifestly clear that Milo is not a boy's dog, insofar as his favorite activities are eating and sleeping (in that order). Luca made up a song when Milo was a chubby puppy that goes, "Milo, precious Milo, sweet and juicy, tender Milo . . ." He still croons it, even though Milo is now the size of an adolescent seal. You can't really hold him in your lap, so Luca lies on the floor, his head on Milo's stomach, and sings to him during television commercials.

On the way home from shopping I tried to counter the misery of trudging along with bags of groceries and freezing toes by conjuring up the memory of lying in the moss of a Minnesota forest, with curly-headed ferns bobbing over my head and a sweet, warm smell of growth and black earth around me.

How I Know I Married the Right Man: Last night we went to the cinema, where we watched the Meryl Streep movie *It's Complicated.* We had to sit separated by two people because of an extraordinarily rude woman, who refused to move over a seat. At first I was cross, but as the movie went on I realized that I was listening to Alessandro laugh, quite as if he were a stranger to me. We laughed — hysterically — at all the same moments. Ordinarily I don't notice, because he's right at my shoulder, but last night I became aware of how great it is to be married to someone whose sense of humor dovetails so precisely with my own.

Back in New Jersey, Father Mahoney wore a black cassock over his majestic stomach, occasionally adding a purple chasuble. In contrast, our priest here is Dior on steroids. Today he wore a white surplice with a foot-long border of handmade lace and a deeply scalloped hem. Over it he wore a crimson brocade chasuble, to which had been appliquéd a dark green velvet cross, adorned with twisting patterns of gold embroidery.

We just came close to a family spat over the question of whether Milo should stay with us in Paris through the spring and be put on yet another diet (which clearly is not going to happen in Italy). Marina said that when we left him in Florence all those years ago, he felt abandoned by us, and that's why he overeats. She's the Oprah of dog owners; I'm sure it will surprise no one that Milo is going home with her for further coddling.

Yesterday I went with a friend to the Musée Jacquemart-André, the home of a nineteenth-century couple who were passionate art collectors. The collection is spectacular; the bath alone was worth the price of entry. My favorite picture was of a dreamy, sensuous young woman by Jean-Honoré Fragonard. A painter stands before her, naughtily drawing her skirt a bit higher with his cane. If you're planning a trip to Paris, this museum is a must-see — the café is catered by a fabulous patisserie, Stohrer. Nicolas Stohrer worked in Versailles as pastry chef to King Louis XV; he's famous for creating the beloved *baba au rhum* (rum cake). Diet suspended for the occasion, I had it, and I think he'd be proud.

I was riveted in the Métro by an utterly superb trench coat worn by a long-nosed Parisian woman in her forties. It was shiny black, stamped with a snakeskin pattern, and belted at the wrists and the waist, with epaulets and large pockets. She wore it with a lacy white scarf and a busman's hat, jauntily situated on the side of her head: Emma Peel from *The Avengers,* with a Gallic flair.

How to Know You've Overdone a Politically Correct Agenda: Anna told me last night, very seriously, that her Italian teacher was racist. Apparently they watched and then discussed *Star Wars* (the educational value of which was lost on me). "You told me that you should never describe people by their race and then say bad things," Anna insisted. So what was the teacher discussing? The alien races in the bar scene.

Le Bon Marché is a department store with a fabulous gourmet grocery section. Imagine a table laden with shallow boxes with fresh, pale brown eggs tumbling out. Surrounding them are egg cartons in Easter egg shades . . . choose your eggs, choose a pastel-colored carton, make a wonderful omelet!

I have decided to adopt a French style of dieting, not including the leek soup. It has become clear that French dinner plates are smaller than American ones, and French people eat very small portions, forgoing seconds. Alessandro is complaining, as I order a full meal and leave him to finish a good part of it. I find that eating two spoonfuls of crème brûlée is infinitely preferable to eating none whatsoever.

Yesterday Anna's class laughed at her when she made a mistake in two-digit multiplication. And Luca slunk through the door with shadows under his eyes, his math test covered in red. The Italian school is far more difficult — and thereby more traumatic — than their former school in New Jersey. Sometimes I can't sleep, wondering if we've done the right thing coming here. My children inherited my (lack of) math ability, and figures are doubly difficult to calculate while speaking Italian.

I tend to think of umbrellas as transitory, expendable objects that pass through my hands, to be left broken in trash cans, left behind in restaurants, left in taxis, cars, airplanes. But of course they weren't always disposable: in the nineteenth century, they were made of silk, ruffled and flirty and intended to shade a lady's delicate skin — and show off her exquisite taste. At an exhibition of historic early umbrellas, it was clear that lace, perhaps two flouncing levels, was au courant.

In the window of Le Bon Marché hang enormous gold birdcages. Fake canaries are poised on perches outside the bars. And the cages hold Louis Vuitton handbags. The biggest cage holds a gorgeous dark marine bag, its surface embossed and shiny. A yellow canary sits outside, head cocked to stare at the bag, which is (presumably) too beautiful to fly free and must live in a gilded cage instead.

Marina said today the first thing she plans to do back in Florence is find a new vet. That nasty vet who told her Milo is obese, she said, is too young and doesn't understand Milo's emotional problems. Taking his life in his hands, Alessandro pointed out that the vet was the third and most recent to cast aspersions on Milo's weight, and that the most important number to keep in mind was not the vets' years, but the figures displayed on their scales.

Going out to dinner, Alessandro and I passed four teenage girls sitting together on a heating grate, carefully tapping the ashes from their cigarettes into the grate, managing to look almost grown-up. But their voices betrayed them, spiraling high into the air with their cigarette smoke, as if those Bon Marché canaries were singing in the cold.

Last night Alessandro and I walked to the cinema. On the way home we passed a man tap-dancing, Duke Ellington pouring from his CD player. He had a hat and long, skinny legs; his feet clicked the pavement of boulevard Poissonnière so quickly that it was as if a spider were dancing in little tap shoes.

I have fallen in love with the shiny tiled walls of the Métro. Most stations have their own distinctive styles, dating back to the original construction, from the look of it. In Madeleine, a line of pearly aqua tiles are sculpted in bas-relief, creating a stylized wave that runs along the passageway. The wave morphs into a complicated "NS" pattern, those initials standing for the Nord-Sud line, as it was labeled in 1900. The Cité station has four-petaled flowers in glossy bottle green. The Concorde station was renovated about twenty years ago, and the huge vault over the tunnel for Line 12 is completely covered with white tiles, each bearing one black letter. It reminds me of when my children, as toddlers, used to jumble up refrigerator magnets in the form of letters. I would crow with exaggerated delight if *cat* was achieved; these tiles, however, are entirely more august: they spell out excerpts from the Declaration of the Rights of Man, from the French Revolution.

I asked if Alessandro would pick up some of the spectacular chocolate mousse made by a patisserie on nearby rue Richer. His response: "I thought you were on a diet." These seven words rank among the more imprudent things he has said to me in the long years of our marriage.

Yesterday, to Anna's delight, Domitilla was unceremoniously tossed out of class and told to wait on a bench until school was over (a few minutes). Alas, today Anna was bounced out of math class to the same bench. I pointed out that perhaps she and

Domitilla were more alike than Anna might want to believe. "So, why were you kicked out of class?" I asked. "Rambunctiousness," Anna answered morosely. "That teacher doesn't understand my sense of humor."

Today I sat at a café and read Claude comparing life in Florence to that in Paris. As he saw it, living in Florence makes a person become witty ("most people do, I believe"). I feel doubtful, given clear evidence to the contrary from my Florentine in-laws. In Paris, Claude writes, one "lives life too fast, like a mouse under oxygen," and is likely to die at thirty. My sister, the font of all genealogical knowledge, tells me that Claude was born in 1884, which means that he was twenty-four or twenty-five when he lived here, and that he lived only to forty-two. Perhaps it was all that Parisian oxygen.

Alessandro just came back from his conversation exchange: Florent is devastated. He logged on to Facebook and discovered that the object of his adoration, the waitress in Italy, had changed her status. She's "in a relationship"! Florent says, dolefully, that she made a point of not telling him in person, and that he is very hurt by her indirect methods. I think that, given his scanty Italian and her nonexistent French, she may never have figured out his passion, let alone his honorable intentions. After all, he didn't employ the romantic phrases that Alessandro taught him.

Paris (and our apartment) is so dark and quiet this morning that I feel as if I'm entirely alone. The sky is the color of gray flannel, the darkness broken only by the dormer window of another early riser. The woman who lives in that attic painted her walls yellow, and reflected light bounces out like a spring crocus. If light were sound, her window would be playing a concerto.

Today we walked by a store window revealing a room full of unclothed mannequins with (as Anna pointed out) nipples, not to mention very idealized figures. They stood around in groups chatting, and demonstrating how they could raise an arm, or twist to the side. Only one mannequin was dressed in a short black cocktail frock and a wig of tumbling curls. She was seated, legs crossed at a rakish angle, and somehow her sartorial, bewigged splendor made the others look fifty times more naked — and erotic.

We started out this year the way any modern

American family would: with multiple cell-phones. But I inadvertently left mine on a table in London months ago, and I haven't replaced it. Life without a phone is riskier, lonelier, more vivid. My family doesn't understand. "What if I have to talk to you?" Anna wails. "We already paid for the contract," Alessandro scolds. I remain obstinately disconnected.

I happened across a protest march organized by the unions that was unlike any I'd ever seen in the United States. The protesters ambled along in little groups, sipping their coffee. There was no equivalent to the "One, two, three" chanting Americans use to stay pumped up. Every fourth or fifth car played music, so in the time I walked along, going the other direction, I heard rock, rap, and finally (from a hospital's association) Handel.

I am trying to teach Anna not to engage with the very pretty, and very pestilent, "Queen Bee" in her classroom. (The girl I have called Beatrice.) Anna tends to fight back, which makes things worse. This morning I asked her if Domitilla was one of the queen's courtiers. It turns out that Domitilla is not a "cool girl," and that those little wasps actually push her around, quite literally. To Anna's horror, I announced that we are having Domitilla over for a playdate.

My favorite statue in Paris is an allegorical grouping, Boisseau's *La Défense du Foyer,* in the Esplanade des Invalides. Alessandro tells me that a *foyer* is a hearth, which explains why Monsieur stands bold and tall, ready to slay dragons, while his wife and child huddle behind him. He has a very nice physique — and he's naked save for an animal-skin loincloth furnished with a suggestively placed paw. To an American eye he looks like an early explorer, especially given his single moccasin, with the important distinction that he has maintained — and trimmed — his luxuriant French mustache.

Anna and I are both down with sore throats — something I blame on the fact that we shivered through two freezing days before the furnace was finally fixed yesterday. She is snuggled next to me, occasionally reading aloud from a Harry Potter book (Anna sees reading as a communal activity). " 'The afternoon sun hung low in the sky,' " she reads, and then tells me, "I like that, because the sun doesn't really hang from anything, and so it's cool." Thank you, J. K. Rowling, for teaching at least one eleven-year-old the joys of figurative language!

We had a playdate yesterday afternoon with Anna's archrival, Domitilla. Ever since Domitilla succumbed to passion and slapped Anna at the beginning of the year, Anna has considered her persona non grata. But lo and behold, the two played happily for hours. "She likes me," Anna reported afterward. "I'm thinking about liking her back."

Luca's New Year's resolution was to pass ninth grade. Translating arcane verb forms from Latin into Italian (which he speaks fluently but conjugates with difficulty); creating detailed architectural drawings; going to one-man plays in French . . . this year is stretching him in ways that he never imagined. He would be the first to tell you that he didn't need any such stretching. But today he aced exams on classical theater and math!

Over the years of raising children I was forced to give up baths for rushed showers, unable even to pee without someone outside the door, wailing. These days, as soon as Anna is in bed, I seek refuge in steaming water. The pages of paperback romances, along with my fingers and toes, wrinkle the way they used to when I was fifteen; my body feels strong, buoyant, unscarred.

This morning Anna and I walked down our narrow little street in the near dark on our way to school. Suddenly a huge flock of starlings swooped down low, flying over our heads between the building to our right and the conservatory to our left, their wings black against the pearly sky. Just before rue du Conservatoire dead-ends in a row of tall buildings on rue Richer, they all turned around and flew back, close enough that we heard the whir of their wings, as if angels swooped down to visit two blocks of a Paris street.

Anna came home from school teary. She was yelled at in French class for misplacing her homework, in Italian class for secretly reading Harry Potter, in math class for flubbing her exercises, and was kept in at recess for berating a boy who wrote her name on the board (it's unclear why he felt moved to do so). "There was one good class," she said, sniffling. "In English, I was the only one who spelled 'The orange bag is in the bedroom' correctly." Forgive me if I don't get too excited.

Anna had a sleepover guest last night, her friend Nicole. They played Monopoly until Nicole said (in French), "Told you I was great!" and Anna answered (in English), "Let's jump on my bed!" This morning I made pancakes, which Nicole promptly rolled up like crepes; Anna followed suit. I am dazzled by the novelty of my daughter's life, but she is not. "When are we going home?" she just asked. "You said a year, and we've been here two years already, easy."

Alessandro and I walked to our covered market today and discovered that the very first narcissus of the year are for sale. They're sweet-scented, pale yellow with bright orange centers, and smell indisputably of spring. We bought some, and when we walked outside, snow was falling. My spring flowers arrived home dusted with a bit of winter.

The right aisle of our church is the province of elderly men seeking handy access to the bathroom. A worthy gray-haired burgher with a generous stomach and a walrus mustache always sits just to the right of the altar. Anyone on his way to the bathroom pauses to shake hands with him and exchange a quiet word. Monsieur la Moustache looks like the mayor in an old French movie: the Mayor of the Men's Room, the Lord of the Lavatory.

When you exit the station at Champs-Élysées, before you reach the commercial end of the street, you walk a long path adorned with a revolving pop culture exhibition presented on huge placards. Earlier this year, there were blowups of vintage *Vogue* covers. Now? Clint Eastwood. It's odd to find the raw western antihero himself gracing Paris's most iconic street.

My father is recovering from a broken hip; wanting to give him something both beautiful and useful, Alessandro and I headed out to Cannes Anciennes de Collection, a cane shop with Chinese canes carved with birds, and antique French canes topped with cheerfully naked nymphs. We found a fascinating walking stick, made for a country vet around 1900. The top unlatches to reveal a secret stick, used to measure the height of a horse. My grandfather was a farmer, and my father still hankers after open fields; this will make him very happy.

■ ■ ■ ■

The Invalides Métro station at 8:30 in the morning smells like buttered toast, which makes me remember my mother, slathering butter onto homemade bread. Today Anna said dreamily, "I love this brand-new croissant smell." I realized that she is creating her own buttery memories, to be recalled decades from now.

As I was walking along the street today, my eye was caught by the gleam of orange berries hanging from two small bushes in pots on either side of the "door" of a pup tent set up on the sidewalk. Inside was a man, his tent flap half unzipped, feeding sparrows at his threshold. *"Bonjour, madame!"* he cried, with such an infectious smile that I waved, realizing only halfway down the block that he might be hungry.

Florent is still disconsolate. Alessandro reports that he had been thinking of taking a leave from his job as a middle school teacher and moving to the town in Italy where the heartless waitress lives. I feel some sympathy as regards her decision. It is extraordinarily difficult to navigate interlingual relationships, especially in the beginning. I couldn't figure out how to pronounce Alessandro's name correctly for at least two weeks after we started dating — far too long to ask him again exactly how it sounded. Luckily a friend visited from England and coached me in rolling Rs. Somehow we survived.

By this point in our sojourn in Paris, we've encountered a number of amiable protest marches. My favorite part is the coda: on the heels of the last ambling protester comes a miniature fleet of four or five green city trucks, the same public-works fellows whose comrades are often found marching at the front. The drivers have a great time doing spins on the car-free avenues while sweeping and washing.

This afternoon Anna walked through the door, her face closed and tight. It turned out that Beatrice is having what promises to be a particularly splendid birthday party, to be held at an indoor water park — but not everyone in the class is invited, and Anna was not one of those anointed ones to be handed a precious invitation. "Right after that, my tummy started hurting," Anna said. Mine, too.

■ ■ ■ ■

Boulevard des Invalides is lined with chestnut trees that lost their leaves months ago, but not all their burrs. The chestnuts hang from curling, fragile stems high in the air, creating knots of black lace against the morning sky.

I have now turned from having rather unwelcome gold highlights to being a blonde. It wasn't a change I wished for or welcomed (though one could say that it's France's revenge for my terrible language skills). Although I like to tell myself that I am not shallow, it turns out I was lying. Hair apparently ranks just below the happiness of my children and possibly above my husband's happiness.

When we moved into this apartment, I first noticed the windows because they are draped in shimmery peacock blue taffeta from the ceiling to the floor — very Parisian, I thought. But over the months I've realized that having five-foot-tall windows through which to view the world changes everything. Watching snow fall on the other side of large panes of glass makes it feel as if the snow falls in the room itself; a normal window brackets off the snow, as if it fell on a Hollywood set, far away.

Alessandro came home with a mischievous expression on his face and an unfamiliar shopping bag in his hand. Inside, the most gorgeous hat I've ever seen, of mossy velvet, with a floppy flower on one side. The brim can curl up like that of a Jazz Age flapper, or rakishly down over one ear. My newly blond (and heretofore despised) hair now looks like a brilliant decision!

I walked past the man in the pup tent again. He has built a little wooden threshold in front of his tent to support his two berry bushes; they are firethorn, perhaps. A small dish discreetly invited assistance; as I bent over to put in a coin, I saw that his tent flap was open. He was inside, sitting in the lotus position, meditating. I walked home thinking how happy he looked, with his orange berries flaring against the gray sidewalk, and his simple house.

Last night Anna and I cooked dinner while Alessandro and Luca wrestled with algebra; there's to be a two-hour test tomorrow. When the pasta was ready, the guys were not, thanks to mathematical complications. So Anna and I sat down to read aloud some Enid Blyton with an appetizer of a crusty baguette, delicious sweet butter, and a twist of salt from the grinder. We ate, and read. And ate. And read. By the time the boys had put the final algebra problems to rest, there was no bread left, and no room in our stomachs for dinner.

Parisian life is small and quiet. I pack the children off to school and then think greedily about how many hours I have before they come home. I have come to the conclusion that silence and time are the most precious commodities.

We wandered through the Hôtel Drouot auction house yesterday, and I fell in love with a fainting couch labeled *"Duchesse à Oreilles, Époque Régence,"* upholstered in a brocaded cream adorned with nodding heads of rosy flowers. I instantly envisioned whole cascades of my heroines gracefully swooning onto this couch.

Parisians stand to the side of an opening train door, waiting for passengers to exit, rather than elbowing their way on. They form neat lines at the grocery store. I seem to be the only jaywalker in the city. But let one of them behind a steering wheel . . . everything changes. Held up in traffic for more than thirty seconds, a Parisian goes berserk and honks until the surrounding buildings shake.

I stood for a while in the freezing cold yesterday and watched an old man play his barrel organ. His huge orange cat slept on top of the instrument, wrapped in a small sheepskin. Tourists kept giving him euros to take a picture, which struck me as so odd. I tried to imagine the slide show back home. "And here is Doris, standing next to the old Frenchman playing an organ."

High up, somewhere in the milky sky, the snow clings together before it pinwheels gently down in little clumps. Thousands of cotton bolls were trying to seed themselves on rue du Conservatoire.

Anna spent last evening rearranging her room. She's divided her shelves into "books with girls in them," "books in which bad stuff happens" (mostly fairy tales), and "books for every day" (Junie B. and Enid Blyton). I took a look at my bookshelves. I have "books with happy endings" and "books telling me how to be happy."

We spent the afternoon at the Musée des Arts et Métiers, a quirky, wonderful science museum in the 3rd arrondissement, housing everything from Regency carriages to an early Apple computer. There's an automaton doll admired by Marie Antoinette (it can play eight tunes!) and the very first satellite, which broadcast to the world Neil Armstrong's steps on the moon. Luca was most fascinated — if slightly freaked out — by the objects such as the iPod that we use now but that have already found a place in the museum.

All my life I've heard of Foucault's pendulum, but I didn't know what it was until we saw an original version at the Musée des Arts et Métiers. The pendulum sweeps over a table, and as the earth turns on its axis, tilting the table ever so imperceptibly, the pendulum swings toward a new position, finally knocking over a small metal block. We watched . . . and watched . . . When the block clattered on its side, I felt, for just a second, as if the earth lurched below our feet.

Mariage Frères, a *maison de thé* that opened

in 1854, will leave you happily wiggling with caffeine. They keep their teas in huge canisters marked with fascinating names. I bought Thé des Poètes Solitaires for my father (a solitary poet), and for myself, Earl Grey French Blue in tea bags. The tea of solitary poets was measured out on big brass scales, and the tea bags turned out to be made of thin muslin.

I took Alessandro to the Musée Nissim de Camondo today. I have decided that my favorite portrait in the collection is Élisabeth-Louise Vigée-Lebrun's *Bacchante* in the large study. Her body is glowing, curvy, nude but for a swath of leopard skin across her lap. Moïse placed another nude woman over his bed, which is snugly tucked in its own alcove. Given his love of paintings of nudes and his membership in a club for epicures, Moïse seems to have been a sensual man — which makes it all the more sad that his wife ran off with an Italian horse trainer. Alessandro insists that because the horse trainer was a *baron,* his nationality and occupation were irrelevant.

Alessandro and I watched the informational video about the history of the de Camondo family and the museum, and I disgraced myself by crying, though surrounded by rows of stoic French people. After Moïse's wife absconded with the baron, he seems to have raised their young children with the flair of a modern stay-at-home dad. But after his only son, Second Lieutenant Nissim de Camondo, was killed in the First World War, he became a recluse; he died in 1935, having donated his house to his adopted country to serve as a public museum. When World War II hit, his only daughter, Béatrice, could not believe that she and her children could be in danger; after all, her father had left his house to the nation, and her brother had given his life defending France. Yet Béatrice; her husband, Léon; and their two children, Fanny and Bertrand, were all sent to Auschwitz. None of them returned. Moïse's fabulous collections, the silver platters commissioned by Empress Catherine II of Russia, the furniture covered with gold leaf, could not buy him the most important possession of all: the safety of his children. Writing this, I have changed my mind. There was no disgrace in my tears.

In the deluxe department store Printemps, I stood on the escalator behind a woman wearing a dusky green coat with velvet lapels . . . and holding a bag. What a bag! It was a tote bag in rose, a kind of dreamy dark pink. It had the same electric effect on me that the Twist'n Turn Barbie did years ago: to see it was to lust after it. I edged up a step, determined to see the label. Goyard. Seemingly more exclusive than Vuitton, in business since 1853 . . . and the King of the Tote.

Alessandro came home from his conversation exchange with Viviane and told me they compared their students, Alessandro's at Rutgers to Viviane's at Université Paris-Est Marne-la-Vallée. Viviane said that hers no longer remember how to spell, whereas Alessandro thinks his were never taught. I, too, have forgotten how to spell. With spell-check at my command, I simply don't bother anymore.

Last night Alessandro and I went to a restaurant full of courting couples (always a charming backdrop), where the champagne tasted like apples. It should have been a perfect evening, but the food was not good. Alessandro's risotto was more like rice soup; my duck was underseasoned; the pear clafoutis was bland and overcooked. Now here's the surprise: it's happened a lot here.

In fact, I would venture to say that a nation of brilliant cooks tolerates a great many pedestrian restaurants — and this one hadn't a tourist in it to excuse its mediocrity.

Luca threw himself on the bed next to me a while ago, and is apparently thinking deep thoughts. "Double-you makes some weird words," he says finally. "Like *waaaarble*." He drawls out the sound. "Plus *wanton* and *wonton*. They sound the same." On reflection, I think that *wonton* is actually a more interesting-sounding word than *wanton*, though you'd never know it to read my novels, given my profusion of wanton heroines.

Today we went to Sunday brunch at one of Gordon Ramsay's restaurants in Versailles, La Véranda. The entrées were fine . . . but the desserts! I tried *nine*, determined to learn, through empirical research, the very best one. The delicious, chewy passion fruit *macaron?* The froufrou hot pink marshmallows, the four flavors of crème, the fig tart, the delicate clafoutis? The winner was a dainty cake with a crackling top and luscious mango cream inside, because it was like biting into one of Alice's Wonderland cakes: inside was a voluptuous surprise.

173

■ ■ ■

In Versailles, we visited the Musée Lambinet, which has a curious, motley collection of household objects from the eighteenth and nineteenth centuries, including a bed built into the wall. Anna plopped herself on the floor beside it, and with her for reference, we decided it couldn't have been much longer than five feet. They also had fascinating brass plates used to print toile fabric. One of the designs, *L'Art d'aimer,* showed a canoodling young couple with a sketchy gentleman peeking through the bushes, nothing like the tame images that show up on toile these days.

My favorite items at Musée Lambinet were two "surprise" Easter eggs, given to Princess Victoire, daughter of Louis XV. They are, essentially, historic Polly Pockets, but made with real hen's eggs. The tops were held on with slender chains. One had a little house scene, with a tiny housewife receiving a visitor. The other was a forest scene. In comparison, Fabergé eggs (which postdated these by over a hundred years) seem gaudy and vulgar.

■ ■ ■ ■

A very modish mademoiselle entered the Métro car just after me: her cherry red coat was trimmed in black and cinched at the waist with a wide elastic belt. She had bleached blond short hair, cat-eye glasses, and a leopard-print scarf over her head. She looked like a chic update of Brigitte Bardot. I was cataloging all this French fabulosity when it dawned on me that she was speaking English! And not just any English — *American* English. Go, red, white, and blue!

After school, Anna met me with a lopsided smile that always means trouble. Apparently at lunch she'd offered her cheese to a boy. Rejecting cheddar as beneath him, he tossed it back; naturally, she threw it at his head. He flung it at another boy, and within seconds the air was full of winged cheese, though the teacher didn't see because he had his back turned. Anna retrieved the cheese and threw it back at the first boy, whereupon it bounced off his shoulder and hit . . . the teacher. Naturally.

This morning I dropped Anna off at school, then walked across the Seine on a lavishly gilded bridge. The wind was fiercely chilly, but the sky bright blue, and the way the sun shone on the river and danced over all that gold leaf opened a door straight from winter to a slice of spring.

Our *gardienne* just came up to deliver the mail. I'm correcting proofs of my latest manuscript, so Alessandro brought Anna to school this morning, and I never bothered to get out of my PJs. Her eyes flickered from my uncombed hair down to my flannel-clad, flowery legs and then back up to my face. *"Bonjour!"* she said cheerily, and I knew that my sartorial choices will have been discussed with every single resident of 15 rue du Conservatoire by this time tomorrow.

Today Luca and Alessandro were out walking and saw a delicate chocolate shoe in the window of Joséphine Vannier, *"Chocolat Artisanal."* They bought it to celebrate my finishing the proofs of *A Kiss at Midnight,* my version of *Cinderella.* Every detail, from the heel to the toe, is astounding — and it is filled with gorgeous little chocolates.

Alessandro has turned himself into a long-distance runner here and regularly goes for forty-minute runs. Last night he was poking at his muscled chest and saying, "Do you think I'm getting scrawny?" At that very same moment I realized my favorite green pants don't fit in the thighs or butt anymore.

Today I went to Luca's high school to give a lecture on Shakespeare and *Macbeth.* Leaving embittering details aside (though I won't forget them till death), let me just say that grades nine through twelve were gathered together in the gym; that some of them had had only a semester of English — though they all had electronic devices; that only one grade had read any Shakespeare at all; and that the head of the school introduced me, concluding with a plea that they behave. After which she handed me the microphone and said *"Buona fortuna."* Good luck!

Anna has leapt into a new role: romantic adviser to the eleven-year-old set. Her ex-enemy, now-friend Domitilla apparently has a crush on a young Star Wars fan. "She wanted to wear her hair in braids over her ears, like Princess Leia," Anna said, shrugging. "But I think he has a crush on Nicole, so he wouldn't even notice. Boys don't." In my opinion, nothing good could possibly come of Princess Leia hair.

■ ■ ■ ■

The perfect comfort food recipe for eleven-year-old girls with sore throats: boil potatoes, peel them under cold water, mash them with a fork and mix in loads of crème fraîche, then season with a little salt and watch for huge smiles. This from a child who would shriek with disgust at the idea of cream entering her mouth.

Luca just left for a weeklong skiing trip with his classmates. I gave him a last-minute lecture — no drugs, no drinking, no sex, and no black diamond slopes — while Anna listened with some fascination. "Why are you telling him all that?" she demanded at the end. "He can't do those things! He's a PG-13, not an R."

An interesting development in Florent's life! During today's conversation session, he apparently didn't even mention the cruel-hearted Italian waitress, but talked the entire hour about a woman he has known for a year and a half, just as a friend. She teaches French language and literature in the same middle school as Florent. He always thought she was interesting but, obsessed by his waitress, had never really considered the possibility. Now he has.

We found a furniture store in the Marais that features curlicues: lampshades with elaborate cutouts; a cabinet with wrought-iron overlay; a sofa whose arms spiral around and around, like a snail's shell. I fell in love with an asymmetrical red velvet chair whose one arm forms a voluptuous curl, while the other flares into a sharp corner. Even so, I find it hard to imagine the person who would want to live with this furniture: she would have to live a life ruled by *le chic*.

CHICKEN SOUP

My mother's trajectory was from riches to rags. She always said that she never learned to cook because she grew up in a household with a cook and several maids. Because these facts about my mother came as I was growing up in a dilapidated farmhouse in rural Minnesota, I was fascinated by the idea that she used to live like a princess.

I badgered her to tell me details; my favorite story was about the time when she hid in the martini cart as it was being wheeled into the living room, tumbled out, and threw up at my grandfather's feet. The highlight of the story for her was the moment my grandfather genially declared that his only daughter was free to vomit wherever she pleased. That detail never interested me — my siblings and I had taken for granted our right to vomit throughout the house. What I wanted to hear about was the martini cart: its rows of funnel-shaped glasses, the gently clinking bottles, the rustle of a starched apron as a maid tenderly served my grandparents their first cocktail of the evening.

There was no getting around the fact that the family fortunes had fallen since those gilded days. Rather than marrying a scion of the banking universe, my mother had inexplicably married a farmer's son; what's more, her groom was a poet, and poetry is a lot harder to sell than corn. Back when my parents were first married, their house didn't even have running water.

As the story goes, my mother — thrown into the deep end and forced to cook or sink — taught herself by working her way right through *The Joy of Cooking*. I never really believed this. It was indisputable that she had mastered oatmeal, pot roast, and a cake she called Never-Fail Cake (the very label suggests the tail end of many a meal). But she spent most of her time cramming my brothers into white shirts for dinner, teaching us how to gently tap a soft-boiled egg perched in a porcelain eggcup, and instructing us in the mysteries of a table set with family silver, which she insisted on using at every meal. In truth, her uncanny ability to ruin a recipe — to give even a Never-Fail Cake a strange metallic taste, for example

— cannot be blamed on Irma S. Rombauer. Mom resented giving it time and energy; inside, she felt cooking was someone else's job. She wasn't even terribly interested in the way food tasted.

I, too, never got over our lost blue-blooded past; eventually that fascination became the hallmark of Eloisa James. If heroines in my romances are not born fantastically rich, they have become so by the final chapter, and — to a woman — they grow up with maids.

Yet one thing I have learned from living in Paris is that even if I were surrounded by starched aprons, I would never trade the patrician life for the ability to cook. Parisians give kitchen work time. In the last six months, I, too, began giving cooking time and energy; I even read some cookbooks. One week I added cumin to everything from eggs to lamb. Some dishes worked; some didn't. I added lavender beads to a chocolate cake (not so good), and vodka to beet soup (very good). I did not spend time learning how to cook applewood-smoked rabbit with truffle oil. I gave time to simple things: risotto, a good broth, comforting soup.

Then we invited over new friends to dinner, including, on one notable night, a banker with an impressively Falstaffian stomach. He is the type of Frenchman who, at least in my imagination, drinks from martini carts and enjoys pigs' feet with green lentils. I gave him chicken soup.

He asked for seconds.

So . . . for those of you who might want to dazzle the Frenchmen in your future, here's my chicken soup recipe:

Lemon Barley Chicken Soup: The first thing you have to do is make chicken broth. Over here in France, I can't seem to find acceptable packaged chicken broth, so I make it from scratch; it's really not tricky. Remove the skin from four or five chicken thighs. Put them in a big pot, along with a cut-up onion, a carrot or two, some celery, salt and pepper, and lots of water. Cook this mélange very, very slowly (bubbles just rising) for a few hours (at least three).

When you've got the broth under way, cook the barley: take 1 cup of barley and simmer it slowly in 4 to 5 cups of water. When it's soft, drain the barley, but reserve any remaining barley water so you can add it to the broth.

When the broth is ready, skim off the froth. Then remove the chicken thighs and when they're cool enough, strip the meat off the bones, saving it for the soup. Strain the broth and put it to the side.

Now that you've got chicken broth, it's time for the soup itself — the rest is even easier.

Cut up some leeks, if you have them, though an onion works just fine, too. If you've got leeks, put some butter in your (now emptied) stockpot over low heat; use olive oil instead if you have onions. While the leeks/onions are softening, finely mince a knob of ginger and 2 or 3 garlic cloves. If you can get some, you can also crush some lemongrass and put it in at this point. I never seem to cook it right (it always stays tough), but it adds great flavor. Dump all that in with the softened leeks/onions. Cook until you can smell it, but take care to avoid browning. Then add the cut-up chicken and the barley, and pour in the broth. Simmer it over low heat for about half an hour. Add salt to taste.

To get a great lemon kick, squeeze 2 lemons and beat the juice well with 2 egg yolks. With the pot removed from the heat source, briskly whisk this mixture into the soup, being careful that the eggs don't separate and curdle. Then return the pot to the heat and stir vigorously for a bit, until the eggs are cooked.

This soup is excellent for sick people (ginger, hot lemon, and chicken; need I say more?) and a tonic for sad people (total comfort). And it's even better the next day.

In Bon Marché: a display of gorgeous designer shoes in jewel tones. Above the shoes hang tiny, extremely fluffy tutus, rather as if snowy white dandelion puffs were floating from the sky.

In France, the state provides free child care when schools are closed for holidays. So yesterday Alessandro brought Anna to our local *centre de loisir* — the center for leisure, or day camp. She clung to his hand, and said afterward that she could feel herself turning white from fear. But she came home joyful, having made three new friends. "When I had to speak French, I did," she told me. "It just burst out of my mouth!"

I was early to pick up Anna at day camp, and so I read all the notices and one plaque mounted outside "in memory of the students of this school deported from 1942 to 1944 because they were Jewish." Apparently more than three hundred children from the 9th arrondissement were sent to the camps; the sign promised *Ne les oublions jamais.*

They will never be forgotten. By the time Anna pranced out, I was tearful, though she didn't notice. The air was warm and smelled like spring, so we sat down at a sidewalk café for a glass of wine (me) and Orangina (her). Anna put a little clay polar bear, made that day, on the table. "His arms and legs fell off," she said, carefully arranging the little blobs next to the body, as in a sacramental funeral rite. "His nose, too," she added, rather dismally.

The berries have fallen from the homeless man's bushes; perhaps this means spring is coming? Today he had his flap slightly unzipped, and we exchanged polite *Bonjours*. I gave him a coin directly, rather than put it in his bowl, which seemed daringly intimate. *"Ça va?"* I asked. "Everything okay?" *"Oui,"* he said. *"Ça va bien."* All is well.

I'm working on an academic article about a 1607 play obsessed with silk taffeta, so I am reading cheap pamphlets from the era, trying to track down fashion trends. I came across this in a little book of English "witticisms": "The owl and the swallow bring in winter and summer, but the nightingale and the cuckoo talk only of the merry time." We should all be more nightingale-like, perhaps;

I can do without the cuckoo.

Anna came home from day camp yesterday with her eyes large and her hands on her hips. "Mama! You shouldn't be sending me to such a place — the teachers are violent!" Upon further inquiry, it did seem that the teachers were lively — she reported that one had "thrown" a chair. Still, from long experience with Anna's dramatic renditions, I suspected that the teacher's chair toppled. "What did the other children think?" I asked. "They didn't seem to notice," Anna reported. Her life is all the more interesting for the things she sees, which no one else even notices.

Paris restaurant alert! A new friend took us to a Lebanese restaurant with vinegary, delicious salad, smoky lamb, and glorious, not too sweet, desserts: gelatin squares colored hot pink and rolled in delicate coconut flakes, baklava that didn't leave fingers sticky with honey. It's called Assanabel, and as a bonus, the stores around it sell Chanel, Gaultier, and Sonia Rykiel.

My great-uncle Claude had a servant named Eugénie who brought him hot water for shaving while he lazed in bed. He also describes her standing around holding a boutonniere while he adjusted his tie. I try to imagine a maid doing the same for Alessandro, and fail. He would hate the intrusion. I could probably tolerate it, myself.

We have young guests coming in a few days, so Anna and I went to a wonderful Japanese grocery store called Kioko to buy her favorite drink, beloved of all children: pale blue soda with a marble in the cap. To open it, you shove the marble into the neck of the bottle, where it makes a huge fizz and by a miracle of engineering gets stuck, unable to go up or down, no matter how much a child shakes the bottle. Which she invariably does.

Alessandro and I just took an interesting walk up toward Montmartre, the red-light district, home to the Moulin Rouge, the cabaret where dancers with impassive faces stand in a line to kick high over the heads of tourists. Passing a sixty-year-old couple arm in arm, I couldn't help but think about how much more tiresome I find it to dress up than I did in my twenties. But how much harder would it be if you were a sixty-year-old transvestite? Carefully powdering a bony nose . . . foundation after shaving . . . the pure ennui of the whole project.

Last night we went to the oldest oyster restaurant in Paris: Brasserie Wepler, established in 1892. It was packed with customers in family groups and on dates; an exquisite young lady who looked as if she'd stepped from a Pre-Raphaelite painting arrived with her poet-look-alike date. They were seated next to an elderly gentleman who dined alone, after shaking hands with all the waiters. Eating those oysters was like diving under the waves, tasting the ocean's wild coolness, its salt, the faintly alien sense of deep water. . . . The food that followed was, alas, decidedly poor. But perhaps, just for those oysters, it was worth the trip.

My college roommate Marion has arrived for a visit with her husband, Lou, and their children. At lunch in a snug little bistro, her two kids and Anna practiced their Harry Potter Quidditch signals. We paid no attention to them until a sudden swell of noise demanded it, and we looked up to see that a cops-and-robbers game had taken over. Appalled, Marion yelped, "No gun play — not in a *French* restaurant!" As if little French boys didn't swagger about using their baguettes as pretend weapons.

■ ■ ■ ■

Anna's grades in French have been miserably low (around 2 out of 10, on an average test). But that week in French camp made all the difference. She came out of school dancing with joy. Her teacher apparently took a look at her test and shrieked, "Oh, my goodness! What happened to you!" Anna got a 9 out of 10, better than anyone in her group. She sang all the way home, and we had steak and ice cream to celebrate.

On rue du Faubourg-Montmartre I suddenly became transfixed in front of a vintage clothing store with the charming name of Asphodèle, which is French for "daffodil." Hanging in the window was a pearly buttercream bag embossed all over with the YSL logo. I could see Jackie Kennedy's gloved hand picking it up, or Catherine Deneuve placing it next to her chair while lunching at the Hôtel de Crillon.

Luca returned from his skiing trip with a big grin. The only glitch was when he crashed his snowboard into a skier, after which he simultaneously apologized in French (to the skier), defended himself in

English (to a critical bystander), and grumbled in Italian to his waiting friends. And just to boost his coolness . . . he hung out with *sophomores.*

Last night Alessandro and I sent our visiting friends out for a romantic dinner alone while we had takeout with all the kids and put them to bed. A bit later six-year-old Sadie woke up, sobbing for her mother. So we talked about how beautiful her mommy looked in her spiffy black dress, all shiny and excited about being in Paris. I sang lullabies, and held her sweaty, sticky-with-tears face against my shoulder, and thought about the fact that in a blink of an eye, Sadie will be singing to her own children.

As I walked down boulevard des Invalides, I could see the homeless man's little bushes dotted with red — and yet I knew his berries had fallen off. I got closer to find that he has hung the bushes with small, bright red Christmas balls. He gestured toward his little trees and laughed: happy to find beauty discarded, or perhaps given to him.

Marion and Lou took us out to dinner tonight. Marion was adamant that we try a restaurant with at least one Michelin star, so Lou and I surveyed the (many) possibilities and chose Stella Maris, which means "star of the sea." The chef is Japanese, and yet the cuisine is French; we thought his star was probably very hard-won. Indeed, the meal was wonderful, though we came to the conclusion that the *amuse-bouches,* of which there were two or three, were better than the entrées. And that no one should spend that sort of money on food.

Apparently the "distinguished professor" look is in high demand in Paris. In the last week alone, a young man leaning in a doorway winked at Alessandro and beckoned; a lonely lady snatched an opportune moment — when I was transfixed by a store specializing in "high heels, all sizes" — to approach him. "Perhaps they think I'm French," he said, preening a little. "Perhaps they think you have a wallet," I said cruelly. His face fell, and I remembered that husbands have tender egos, even if they garner their compliments from unlikely places.

We rented our apartment in part because of its flowery moldings; we had no idea that among its attractions was the fact that it was precisely two blocks away from the oldest *confiserie,* or candy shop, in Paris: À la

192

Mère de Famille, founded in 1761. This is a feast for the eyes as much as the palate: delicate crystallized violets, pastel sugar eggs, and darling marzipan apples, sized for a doll's tea party — or a sweet nibble in the Garden of Eden.

Yesterday I watched as Marion gave six-year-old Sadie the "runway look" that Sadie had picked out from a large eye-shadow palette. Marion's finger brushed pale pink, and she stroked it over Sadie's eyelid. "Now a little smoky blue at the corners," she murmured, dipping her finger into the pink again. She peered down at the instruction card Sadie had chosen. "A little more blue . . ." She rubbed a little more pink at the corner of Sadie's shining eyes. "There, you look gorgeous!" And she did, runway ready, without a touch of color on her eyelids. "You're so good at this, Mama," Sadie said — and I could scarcely disagree.

The homeless man must have a florist admirer! Today he has two new bushes with red berries, like shiny kidney beans.

A Parisian Spring

Spring has come to Paris! The sky before my study window is pale blue, with airplanes' fleecy vapor trails patterning it like lace, and the building across the street is gleaming in the sunshine. The itinerant brass quartet that occasionally plays in our quartier for money is down on the corner tootling "Blue Moon" with great verve but not such great timing.

Anna came out of school with her mouth tight and miserable. Each day one student gets to ring the dismissal bell, and today was Anna's turn. So she dashed downstairs, so excited that she didn't think to ask for permission; she just rang that bell. It wasn't time yet, so she was yelled at and thrown out of the office, and — worst of all — a boy named Tommaso laughed at her.

Yesterday I saw a quintessentially French

umbrella in a shop window: bright red polka dots with a ruffle. I could just imagine that cunning ruffle dancing down a rainy street. I bought it for Anna, only to be asked (with outrage): "Mama! Do you think I'm Minnie Mouse?" If on a wet day you see a quintessential Minnie walking down rue du Conservatoire, *c'est moi.*

Today young men stood outside the Métro stations selling bundles of small narcissus, their stalks tied together very tightly so the heads burst into exuberant posies. Almost every woman handed over a couple of euros, so the street was filled with women holding bright yellow flowers to their noses, looking happy.

At lunchtime Alessandro and I strolled over to a Hôtel Drouot auction preview featuring vintage haute couture, that is, designer clothing made completely by hand. I tried on a Chanel opera jacket that must have weighed fifteen pounds, thanks to the exquisite, heavy gold embroidery and beading — thousands and thousands of tiny hand stitches and shining bright beads. For just a moment, I felt like Grace Kelly.

Florent is the epitome of a romantic Frenchman. Alessandro reports that he is head over heels in love again. It's as if the Italian waitress never existed. Now all he talks about is his colleague, whose name is Pauline. Apparently she is interested but evasive. Florent is forty-one and very much wants to settle down; Pauline is only in her twenties and not ready for a long commitment. Alessandro pointed out that the waitress was quite a bit younger, too, to which Florent retorted that his father is seventy-one and married to a thirty-five-year-old. Hmm.

In Bon Marché, I came across a display of spring shoes in pale yellow and melon. The best were tender pink boots with small silver buttons, and a pair of kitten heels by Sonia Rykiel that sported a glossy bunch of black grapes. They were utterly impractical, and utterly delicious. I wandered from shoes to clothes and stopped before a skirt, the kind that's a bit stretchy. In a fit of spring fever, I decided to try it on — but in the dressing room, it hugged my bottom in a rather distressing fashion. The young salesgirl's face fell when I asked her for a bigger size: "They don't come any larger than that," she said. I slunk out, feeling too bottom-heavy to live in Paris.

■ ■ ■ ■

Marina called from Florence to report that Milo had suddenly toppled off the couch. After some consternation on the part of herself and all her neighbors, they determined that he had a digestive problem. Charcoal was suggested as a remedy. On the first attempt at administering it, via a prosciutto delivery system, Milo gobbled the prosciutto and spat out the hidden charcoal; ditto the second attempt. The third offering, however, was devoured whole. He hasn't fallen off the couch since. Now you know what to do if you ever fall off the couch.

In the Métro this morning: two teenagers entwined behind a beverage dispenser. Anna turned around to ogle them as we walked by. "Their mouths are connected," she hissed, "just like the way married people do." A moment later she added: "Romantic. But disgusting."

My friend Carrie and her daughter Charlotte bounded off the plane yesterday, and before I knew it, I was walking with them all the way up to Montmartre, the highest point in the city. I staggered up the last steps to find the Sacré-Coeur basilica's dome gleaming in the sunlight, covered by rows of creamy scallops that reminded me of children's drawings of ocean waves: very regular, quite fantastic.

When I left the States, stockings were out of style, so I was surprised to find French women sitting at cafés, their glossy legs looking quite fabulous. Carrie and I ventured into a hosiery store and were just informed that this year ladies are wearing "invisible" or "sand"-colored stockings. I find bare legs tiresome, so hallelujah!

Paging Dr. Freud: Me, at breakfast, to Alessandro: "The catacombs sound so interesting! In 1741, a man wandered off, and his body wasn't found for nine years. Let's take the children this afternoon." Moment of silence . . . then gales of laughter. We're going.

Back in 1786, the French emptied a few cemeteries into the catacombs under Paris, marking the entry with a macabre sign: STOP! THIS IS THE EMPIRE OF DEATH. In the catacombs, bones are set into the walls that line winding paths, with long bones and skulls arranged in pretty patterns. There's even a romance writer's delight — a wall constructed of piled femurs interspersed with skulls in the shape of a heart.

The children loved the catacombs. What with squealing at water trickling from the ceiling (possibly French sewers dripping on their shiny hair) and shuddering if they'd accidentally brushed a bone, the subterranean burial site turned into a Parisian treat. Plus, a lively discussion of how one could steal a bone, if one were criminally minded, followed by speculation about lifelong haunting by a vengeful eighteenth-century ghost, cheered everyone to no end.

Carrie and I met a lovely group of French romance readers who showered us with gifts and then took us to a restaurant that had never seen a tourist. We were particularly fascinated, then, by a painting of a young lady wearing nothing but an apron, stockings, and a fetching little hat, and carrying a provocative duster — it was very interesting to see that the French-maid fantasy has the same naughty currency here as in the American male psyche.

Yesterday was a little rainy, and we were

virtually alone in Fontainebleau, the hunting palace of French kings and Napoleon. I stood for a long time looking at Marie Antoinette's gorgeous private boudoir, paneled with glossy, fantastic arabesques . . . at the splendid bed she ordered but never slept in, because the revolution commenced before the royal family returned to the palace. While Versailles is grand and remote, it had made me feel every inch a Norwegian peasant. Fontainebleau, though, made me want to be a queen — though perhaps one with a longer life span than poor Marie.

We wandered into a restaurant at Fontainebleau yesterday; with a wild glint in his eye, Luca ordered pigs' feet with mustard sauce. Then a minute after his plate arrived, he snatched my wonderful lamb. So I cautiously ate the porky trotters, whose ankles must have been chubby indeed, given the fatty meat clinging to their tiny bones. Thank goodness for the excellent Bordeaux.

Fontainebleau has a carousel that matches its royal palace: a double-decker whose horses, tiger, and Cinderella carriages are decorated in ornate pastel arabesques. Carrie and I climbed into an egg frothing with rosy curlicues and went around and around, sedately rocking back and forth while the children threw themselves into a spinning egg. We leaned forward, watching Fontainebleau slide by as if we waved from a royal coach; the children's screaming laughter came on the wind.

Chanel's spring theme seems predicated, oddly enough, on barnyard references. The mannequins in Printemps's windows are posed in front of hay bales, and I just walked by the Chanel store near the Madeleine to find mannequins in short skirts awkwardly clutching rakes. Could it be a response to the recession, a daring (if unconvincing) claim that the ultimate Luxury-Is-Us label is dressing down on the farm?

Strolling out of the ultraluxurious Hôtel de Crillon: a woman, at least sixty, wearing over-the-knee boots (Puss in Boots style, with the tops turned up), a flash of glossy thighs in pale stockings, and a severely seamed skirt. A silk scarf sporting bright orange polka dots floated back over her shoulder.

Today, Carrie, Charlotte, Anna, and I tumbled into Le Dôme, a café on rue de

Rivoli, and were driven by loud music into the back room, which turned out to be fascinating: a louche setting of velvet couches and low tables with metal lanterns that sent out twinkling spills of light. One could just imagine that decayed glamour at night, when swivel-hipped young Frenchmen with earrings lounge on purple cushions.

Carrie and I left our children behind and went for a swishy lunch near place de la Madeleine, around the corner from Chanel and Hédiard. The people eating with us were as fascinating as our scallops: a newborn baby dressed in soft mint-colored linen; a lady sharing a meal with her husband (or lover?) while wearing a pleated silk skirt that fell to her knees, her sweater embroidered in the same pattern as her skirt.

Anna had a tummy ache in class and cuddled with the teacher for most of the hour. I was suspicious of that stomachache, insofar as Anna is positively Machiavellian at malingering. Domitilla apparently put her head down on her desk and wept loudly because Anna wasn't sitting next to her. "She's so dramatic," Anna complained, "and sometimes I still think about the way she slapped me, so I stayed with the teacher."

Yesterday we flew to Florence for Easter with the family. I knew I wasn't in Paris anymore when the entire dinner conversation revolved around food: salami from Sicily (is it better than that from Abruzzi?), the tomatoes bought from a special purveyor, the prosciutto made from "happy pigs" (i.e., free-range pigs, if such a thing is possible). "Any kind of prosciutto makes Milo happy," Anna pointed out. There is no evidence that his current diet has reduced his waistline.

Florence's store windows are full of Easter eggs — tiny ones wrapped in shiny gold foil, some as big as a small poodle, complete with pink bow. My favorites are speckled pigeon eggshells, carefully drilled and filled with molten chocolate. You crack the side with a spoon as if opening a soft-boiled egg, and voilà, chocolate delight.

To Marina's great distress, when she called "Treat, treat!" (Milo's favorite word) this morning, no Milo appeared. Convinced he was dead, she rushed around the apartment looking for him — only to discover him in the living room, stuck behind the couch like a cork in a bottle. Now the couch is pulled a good ten inches from the wall so that Milo's stomach will not be impeded on its rush to the kitchen.

Anna and I went out with Alessandro's aunt for a ladies' lunch today. Anna danced into the Rivoire, an august and elegant institution here in Florence, wearing gorgeous new ballet flats and a ruffled dress. The waiter brought us paper napkins, and then suddenly an elderly gentleman at the next table barked "Filippo! Bring these ladies proper napkins; they are Florentines!" Filippo returned apologetically with huge pale pink linen napkins. We ate like (Florentine) duchesses.

Alessandro and I ventured forth in search of chocolate eggs, since the Easter Bunny finds American children no matter where they happen to be. Generally speaking, the Easter Bunny hops over Italy, where instead parents give big chocolate eggs that crack open to reveal a surprise toy. We saw one the size of a seven-pound baby, decorated with a lush three-dimensional bouquet of chocolate flowers.

■ ■ ■ ■

I always thought boys' reluctance to speak about their feelings was programmed by culture (nurture, not nature) and raised Luca accordingly. But lately he only grunts when asked questions about his emotions. "I can talk about my feelings," he said today, when pinned down. "But" (with unmistakable revulsion) "*not* with my mom." I do hope whomever he's sharing all those feelings with appreciates the effort I put in.

Milo looks very odd when he runs. His legs look like delicate twigs scissoring below his round and furry belly. But he rarely runs anywhere; he avoids even walking whenever possible. He's like a bolster pillow auditioning to be a dog.

Today we went to a small fair that had taken up Easter residence in Florence's biggest park. It was a small, tattered, and supremely illegal carnival: emblazoned with Walt Disney characters, though the magic and copyright-sensitive hands of the Disney corporation surely never came near it. Anna, who had triumphed over the Tower of Terror at Disneyland Paris, found herself petrified by this ancient Ferris wheel. We rose up in the air, sitting in a little car with open sides and no seat belts, and Anna buried her head in her lap and wailed, "This isn't safe! I wouldn't take my daughter on this ride!" I ignored her, enjoying the grin of Thomas O'Malley the Alley Cat on the canopy over my head as we rose into the blue sky, swaying gently.

A delightful Easter memory from yesterday: ladies walking to church holding little bowls tied up in linen tea towels and topped with taffeta bows. Inside were hard-boiled eggs, on their way to Mass to be blessed by the priest. We brought ours home and sliced them, per paschal tradition, into homemade broth, which created a sunny, blessed soup.

Today we all have chocolate hangovers. First the Easter Bunny arrived, then Nonna gave both children foot-high chocolate eggs topped by flares of shiny foil. Then relatives began to arrive — also bearing eggs. The living room table is now full of them, as if someone were growing huge radishes with garish foil tops.

We are throwing a birthday party for

Alessandro's beloved aunt Giuliana, the widow of his paternal uncle, whom she met thanks to being related to his father — after said uncle divorced his first wife. The dinner, which will take place in her favorite restaurant, includes family from both sides, several of whom maintain hostile relations. We just made up the seating chart, which took several hours and is a miracle of strategic and diplomatic finesse, in hopes of avoiding Italian fireworks.

If you ever visit Italy, do not skip the grocery chain Esselunga. They often carry onesies made by the French company Petit Bateau, with adorable little illustrations on the front. I always pick up a few for last-minute gifts, but only after living in Paris have I realized that they are actually cheaper in Italy than on their native soil.

The birthday party for Giuliana went off without a hitch. The children had every reason to behave during dinner, given that my personal threat of evisceration was accompanied by permission to bring books and iPod Touches. For five hours and six courses, they did a pretty good job of pretending to be polite and obedient. But when the birthday cake was delivered, Anna suddenly disappeared. Next thing I knew she was on Giuliana's lap, smiling her most charming grin while a forest of cameras flashed and Giuliana blew out her birthday candles.

Next to our table was another such birthday celebration. Center stage was a pencil-thin, elegant woman with bleached blond hair, fabulous high heels, and a short blue dress. She stood out among her family members like a show poodle sitting in a group of cheerful, loving dachshunds. My favorite moment was when one of her family gave her a floppy messenger bag adorned with a big Snoopy. She charmingly slung it over her shoulder — for the very last time, I'd bet my firstborn.

I went for a run with Alessandro and then trotted up 108 steps to the sixth floor, fell through the door, and threw myself on the living room rug to recover. Milo hauled himself up from his velvet cushion and came to see what was happening. To everyone's delight, he aligned his fat little body next to mine and rolled over on his back so that we could pant in tandem.

Anna's favorite moments in life come when

Luca deigns to play with her. This afternoon Luca played king, sprawled in a chair, while Anna danced about him, waving her wand. Anna, as has perhaps been deduced, is a Harry Potter addict, while Luca prefers the Middle Ages. From the other room, I heard "Avada Kedavra!" (the killing curse), followed by a fifteen-year-old's bellow: "What do you mean, you killed my court poet?"

Today the kids and I went to the Parco delle Cascine, a huge former estate that is now a public park sporting Florence's biggest weekly outdoor market, with stands selling everything from wastepaper baskets to vegetables to dresses for a euro or two. It's a particularly great place to find long translucent curtains, embroidered with flowers or fleurs-de-lis, the emblem of the city of Florence.

Thanks to an Italian hairdresser, my blond hair has been turned bright orange. Alessandro grinned and observed: "It's really different." My bruised self-image was soothed by Luca, who said, "Wow, no suburban moms have hair like that." In an instance of truly regrettable timing, this week Alessandro and I are off to Venice, where I am to deliver an academic lecture before Shakespeare professors. I can guarantee that none of them will have hair that Ronald Mc-Donald would envy.

Yesterday we wandered around Florence, ending up in a fabulous ice cream shop, Gelateria dei Neri, on Via dei Neri, behind Piazza della Signoria. If you ever come to Florence, try the sweet and slightly nutty ricotta and fig flavor.

In Venice for the conference, the first thing we did after leaving our hotel was go to Caffè Florian in Piazza San Marco. When Alessandro and I were grad students and poor as church mice, we shared a tiny pot of tea here for 7,000 lire ($3.50 at the time — a small fortune). Now we had a pot of tea each, listening to a jazz quartet play "And I think to myself, what a wonderful world." Our tab came to thirty euros, or about $44.00, a ha'penny compared to the joy of being there together, solvent and happy.

Today we took a tour of Venice's Jewish quarter. It's the oldest ghetto in the world (dating to the early sixteenth century) — a tiny island where all Jews were compelled to live, so they built houses eight stories high, with no elevators. The synagogues are beautiful, as is the memorial depicting the train that transported people to the concentration camps. Out of hundreds of Venetian Jews, only eight returned. It is heartbreaking.

Venice is like the dream of a sleeping shopaholic — the little, gorgeous footbridges rise into the air and come down into yet other streets of shop windows, shining with gold, velvet, and glass. The streets blend together as if one were wandering in circles, always presented with more to desire, more to buy.

Today I happened on a large pink sign for the Fortuny Museum. I thought vaguely of silk and decided to investigate. Mariano Fortuny (born 1871) was a brilliant fashion designer who worked with finely pleated silk and lustrous velvet. Don't miss this museum: it's a bit gloomy inside, but there's a velvet couch to rest your tired legs and read the museum catalog.

Venice is big, labyrinthine, and full of stairs. Its address system is obscure to the point of impenetrability, and because it has no streets, you can't simply fall into a taxi, which is my response to being lost in other cities. Today I got lost, but then found myself again at the Grand Canal Restaurant at Hotel Monaco. I splurged on an exorbitant lunch on the terrace, by myself. I ate a grilled octopus salad and fish soup *profumo di zafferano,* or saffron, along with a glass of champagne. My waiter thought I was crazy because I drank champagne alone while reading a book. But by that point I was tired of beauty, and a novel set on a foreign planet featuring a cowboyesque hero was exactly what I needed.

My least favorite moment in the academic conference for which I traveled to Venice: an enormously skilled actor performing a scene as a mountebank, or Renaissance con man. He waved his tiny bottle of "Dew of Venus" at my orange hair and said, "For ladies who are going gray, *this* will give you back your auburn tresses." I laughed but thought bitter thoughts about the Italian hairdresser who'd promised to restore my blond hair to its normal red.

On our return to Florence, Marina announced with triumph that while we were in Venice, she'd found a good veterinarian, not like that scoffing fellow who jested at Milo's waistline. This new vet reportedly said that it wasn't Marina's fault that Milo has become a twenty-seven-pound Chihuahua — it was *our* fault because we'd had him fixed. "Neutered dogs are all obese," Marina informed me. In vain did we protest that America is a nation of normal-weight, healthy dogs missing some dangling bits. We fly back to Paris tomorrow, which is probably a good thing in terms of family harmony.

Anna came home and said, "Domitilla and I are best friends now!" This was indeed interesting news. "How did that happen?" I asked. "Domitilla was kicked out of class again, so I raised my hand and asked if I could go to the bathroom. Then I went into the hall and gave her my tiny pink hamster, and now" — Anna said confidently — "she loves me." I'm afraid that bad lessons are being taught by the transactional basis of this new rapport, but I couldn't figure out how to express that intuition without seeming negative.

As I make my way through Claude's memoir about Paris, it is dawning on me that I probably wouldn't have liked him much. He thought that a "spontaneous sense of humor" was rare in a woman. Even worse, he

213

declares that feminine charm is nothing more than bait: there are "steel springs beneath." Dr. Freud would have had a lot to say about those "steel springs *beneath.*"

OF BREASTS AND BRAS

Men have a special relationship with their penises. They name them, they compare them, they spend quality time readjusting their trousers. I haven't seen many women turning their breasts into secret best friends, even those who wryly refer to them as "the girls."

For most of my life, I have considered my breasts to be fully satisfactory: they fed my infant children and were remarkably useful in bed. That measured approach was reflected by my lingerie drawer. By my twenties, it held a motley assortment, unadorned cotton mixing with silky bits of lace, designed for nights in which someone might want to tear off my lingerie with his teeth. Those bras were the Mapplethorpe photos of my bra collection: labeled "explicit" and reserved for special shows guaranteed to inspire a heated reaction.

Over time, marriage, and — regrettably —

cancer, my wisps of lace and satin disappeared through attrition, gradually replaced by sports bras, nursing bras, and the frightening "mastectomy" bra, which has all sorts of inserts. After my breast reconstruction, I became obsessed by organic cotton bras, as if excising synthetics from my wardrobe — as my cancer had been excised — would make me a healthy person, organic from the outside in. My favorites were two identical cotton bras that started out red but, after a few go-rounds in the laundry, faded to bricky pink. They sagged, but my beautifully reconstructed breast did not, so poor construction seemed unimportant.

Then, as they say, came Paris. In the history of my life, this year in Paris might as well be termed the Year of the Brassiere. At some point I walked into the lingerie department at Galeries Lafayette and shamelessly eavesdropped on a conversation between a saleswoman and a client, a very elegant, restrained woman *d'un certain âge,* perhaps sixty-five or seventy. Madame liked the design of a delightful handful of cream silk embroidered with black roses, but if it were not possible to buy panties that matched, then obviously the bra was not for her. It occurred to me that it was entirely possible that a lusty, equally elegant Parisian male, also of a certain age (or younger!), waited for her at home, but more important, *his opinion would make no difference to her.*

She was dressing for herself. And her standards were high. I turned back to the rows of bras and tried to look at them through French eyes: as delicious, delightful accoutrements that would make my breasts look like confectionary pieces — for my own appreciation and pleasure. I swept up a handful and took them into the changing room. Some minutes later, I regarded myself adorned in soft tulle and silk. The straps were twisted together with tiny gold threads, making me feel like a Roman senator's wife. I bought that one, and another of pleated fuchsia silk, and a third in navy, scalloped along the edges.

It scarcely needs to be said that Alessandro celebrated this development; for my birthday he gave me an exquisite bra in cherry red lace. Dangling from a tiny bow was an engraved locket with just enough room, he pointed out, for a photo of him. I could keep my husband next to my heart. (Or between my breasts, however you want to think of it — this may be a gendered consideration.)

In time I accumulated quite a collection of bras, and the panties to match, of course.

And I had also accumulated an extra ten pounds. Ordinarily, that dismaying fact would have made me eschew the mirror. But my Parisian lingerie drew my eyes away from imperfections, and directly to curves enhanced by lace and discreetly ingenious padding. American women may spend their time hating their waists and their hips, but it's my guess that French women spend the same time admiring their breasts — and their hips — no matter their size.

Somewhere in the midst of this feverish period of lingerie acquisition, Anna announced that she was the proper age for a bra. I clearly remember asking my mother for a "training" bra. She snorted, and asked me just how I was going to keep those wild animals in check without training. That unappreciated pun gave way to a speech asserting that breasts and bras were "used by men to keep women in the kitchen" — in retrospect, an explanation that neatly dodged the whole issue of lust. Liberation from the kitchen (and a bra) led to my being the only girl in the sixth grade to find herself naked from the waist up during a scoliosis test — and lo, these many years later, I still feel a surge of resentment at the memory. Consequently, I greeted Anna's request with jubilation: she was becoming a woman and we would have fun, fun, *fun* buying her first bra. She eyed me. "It's not as if I said I was going to have a baby," she pointed out.

Ignoring this deflating remark, we sailed out in search of a training bra. Le Bon Marché proved to have an entire wall of such bras (with matching panties, *naturellement*). Anna focused instantly on a concoction that was scalloped and lacy and altogether French. She snatched it off the hook and clutched it to her nascent bosom, like a crazed shopper at a closeout sale.

It could be that French mothers refer to these tiny scraps of lace as "training" bras. But if so, the training is quite different than what my mother envisioned. As I see it, a French girl is trained to love her figure, and to take personal pride in her clothing, even if that clothing is never intended to be seen by anyone other than the owner (and her *maman*). Put another way, *these* artworks are not designated for gallery shows sure to be outlawed in certain communities: they are not for wild oats, but for private glamour.

At home, Anna tried on her bra and panties and then — as customary whenever new clothing came her way — headed to the living room to model before her father and brother. I grabbed her arm just in time. "Lingerie is private," I told her. "You're a woman now, remember?"

She frowned for a moment, registering that fact, and then she turned back to the mirror.

Alessandro came home triumphant from the market, with the very first peaches of the season. Mine was small with a moody flavor somewhere between sweet and sour — yet every bite celebrated peachiness, a flavor that speaks to one's mouth of summer days so hot that a haze hangs in the air, of iced tea, thick grass, and white eyelet-lace frocks.

I have a lot to do. Revisions for an academic article are due back at the end of this month. I have a column due to the Barnes & Noble Review website addressing five novels. I've promised my editor the first hundred pages of my "Beauty and the Beast" romance, and told my university that I would finish my academic book by June. So I spent the day working on a novella for which I have no contract, no publisher, and no deadline. Alessandro rolled his eyes.

The Petit Palais is offering an Yves Saint Laurent retrospective, so my cousin Laura and I waited in line to see it. I had no idea that YSL popularized the pantsuit, having decided that women ought to stand shoulder to shoulder with men in the boardroom. Or that said pantsuit (perkily pinstriped and worn with a tie) created such a furor. Apparently a socialite, barred entry to a restaurant in New York City because she was in pants, stripped off the trousers and sauntered in wearing only the jacket.

I am particularly fascinated by the Yves Saint Laurent collections in which he appropriated motifs from art. He created a dress using Mondrian's boxy color squares, and a Van Gogh "irises" jacket that must have required weeks and weeks of embroidering beads, sequins, and tiny ribbons to re-create the painting. Laura and I agreed that it was exquisite, though we weren't sure on what occasion one would wear it. "It's my birthday, and I'm wearing a Van Gogh"?

My favorite part of the Yves Saint Laurent exhibition was a towering wall displaying each and every tuxedo he designed in his long career. He was twenty-two when he presented his first collection, in 1958, and it was interesting to see the fifties evolve to the hipster sixties, shoulder pads swell for the eighties, slinky silk appearing in the nineties. Even better: the wall sign informing us that the tuxedos were meant to be "worn with bear skin." I always thought fur beat naked flesh.

Alessandro reported today that Florent is much more in love with his colleague Pauline than he ever was with the Italian waitress. "After all, they can talk to each other," he said. "That's important, don't you think?" It's generally agreed that communication is an essential part of a relationship, yes.

A string of pet shops occupies a couple of blocks along the Seine. Oddly enough, we have visited every shop on two occasions, and haven't seen a single poodle. As in Italy, chipmunks are popular pets. They look (to me) quite dismal, but perhaps Brazilians seeing parrots in cages rather than flashing through trees feel the same.

Yesterday Anna burst into tears at bedtime, saying she had no friends, no one laughed at her jokes, and that she was failing school (her report card indicates otherwise). I pulled out a Gryffindor key chain I had been saving for just such an emergency, and she cheered up while telling me why she was definitely a Gryffindor and not a Slytherin.

In the apartment above us, workers are prying up the original 1760s floorboards only to replace the same boards in such a way that they won't squeak. It was a bad day for us when each board shrieked from its place. But in quieter moments, I hear workmen singing, sometimes Portuguese love songs and sometimes the Muslim call to prayer.

Paris is in bloom! Early this morning I walked down boulevard des Invalides. Flowering trees from the Invalides park were hanging over railings, first one with ruby red buds, and then another with fluffy pale pink blossoms, touched with white, as if sprinkled with icing sugar.

This morning as we entered church, a worthy Frenchman with a huge gray mustache looked meaningfully at Luca's uncombed and wildly curly hair. Once inside, I realized that no other parent had managed to corral anyone over eight, and I couldn't help thinking that the mustachioed gentleman should come over one Sunday early and try to pry a fifteen-year-old out of bed.

I have given up elegance in exchange for attendance.

We have friends visiting from Los Angeles, two artists and their six-year-old daughter, Phoebe. Proud that we could boast near-California-like sunshine on Sunday, we wandered about the markets, and Phoebe bought a bag of French guinea pig food to bring home to her classroom pet, Roxie. Showing true Parisian flair, it's colored like the rainbow. We had a great time at the bird market on Île-de-la-Cité talking to wildly intelligent parrots, until disaster: a box of baby bunnies, tiny bundles of soft fur with sweet floppy ears and pink noses. Phoebe and Anna were both overwhelmed by desire. I explained that, without passports, these bunnies couldn't become U.S. citizens. Showing an early aptitude for a life of crime, Anna pointed out she could hide one in her pocket. "Or my pants," she added.

Today we ran into Anna's friend Nicole's mother, who had her gorgeous two-month-old baby with her. Anna and I hung over the pram while the baby grinned, wide-eyed and toothless, and told us emphatically (in baby language) all about her life. I couldn't help thinking about baby Barbara, in *Mary*

Poppins, who promises the sparrow that she will never forget the language of sparrows and trees. And when she forgets, he cries.

This afternoon we wandered around the Clignancourt flea market admiring (but not buying) vintage Chanel, until our six-year-old visitor, Phoebe, saw a battered purple straw hat. After some fierce bargaining, she pranced happily away. And we all suddenly realized that in her chic boater, Phoebe now looked like a French kid, slumming among Americans.

Anna had a tough time at school today with Beatrice's gang of mean girls, who took possession of the mats during gymnastics class and demanded a password (which, of course, they wouldn't share). On the way home we talked about friends and how complicated they are, and then on the Métro Anna grinned and said, "I have a friend," holding up the fifth Harry Potter book. I remember those days very well. I had friends too: Anne of Green Gables, Dorothy Gale and Toto, Nancy Drew.

Today we all went to the marionette theater in the Jardin du Luxembourg. The first four rows are reserved for children, so that their favorite puppet, Guignol, can ask their advice. In this particular production, duffle-headed Guignol was the servant to a be-wigged aristocrat. "What's the matter, *les enfants?* What's happening?" he would ask. They all shrieked back, warning him of the crocodile sticking its head out of his soup pot. We were seated beside a family with a small, bespectacled girl, who called out advice to Guignol in a piping voice — until a fuzzy spider descended over Guignol's bed and she began screaming instructions. At intermission, she turned to our guests from California and quite politely asked what they thought of the play. They explained (through Alessandro) that they didn't speak French. She thought about that for a moment and then asked: "Why not?"

A French friend steered us to a wonderful food fact: the grocery stores carry fresh gaz-pacho, right next to the milk. If you're going to be in Paris and fancy a picnic, buy a baguette, cheese, and a carton of gazpacho. You can drink it straight from plastic cups, and even in such unrefined containers, it will give your picnic a gourmet flair.

Today we took our guests back to the Jardin du Luxembourg, planning to rent a toy sailboat for Phoebe and perhaps one for Anna. But they turned out to be enticing, and we ended up with four: a pirate ship with the skull and crossbones for Luca, a sail flaunting a pink fish for Anna, a Mary Poppins boat for Phoebe. And the fourth? Phoebe's dad, who's forty-eight, reverted to his eight-year-old self and ran around the pond with a long wooden stick, poking his boat to make it go faster. The garden was packed with all the sorts of people you'd expect to find in a city park on a sunny day, yet no one sat on the grass. No one stripped naked, or played loud music, or tried to entice others to lose their money. We went to lunch in the park's café, drank white wine in the sunshine, and talked about how the French often appear to be the happiest people on earth, though I have no idea whether they actually are.

Luca returned from school with a funny grin . . . sex ed day, French-style! He'd been sent home with an informative cartoon booklet. Anna was fascinated by a page entitled "It's All Normal," which showed a string of girls in an array of shapes and sizes. "Those look like your breasts, Mama. Perhaps I'll have those. But that girl there, she has Grandma's breasts — see how much bigger they are? Maybe I'll have those!" It was window shopping for the prepubescent.

When one is stuck with orange hair, thanks to a bad hairdresser, the only way to surmount the crisis is with aggressive style. I have resorted to a rather severe Victor/Victoria look. Yesterday I bought a pair of elegant, narrow eyeglasses, and then impulsively got a pair of Fendi sunglasses as well. I apparently look like a local; on the walk home I was asked for directions three times. None of which I could answer, alas.

Last night Alessandro and I ambled toward Montmartre, finding ourselves in a street specializing in two things: guitar shops and strip clubs. As the guitar shops seemed to be frequented by fervent, young would-be musicians, financial considerations suggest that the clientele of the two rarely overlap. One of the strip clubs, called Venus, was followed quickly by another called Eve. We peeked through the glass door of yet a third all-but-empty club and saw a woman waiting by the bar for customers. She wore a platinum wig so straight and smooth that it looked like an old-fashioned, tinted photograph of Niagara Falls.

■ ■ ■ ■

I am very fond of the larger-than-life sculpture of Winston Churchill found on the avenue bearing his name and inscribed with WE SHALL NEVER SURRENDER on its plinth. The sculptor, Jean Cardot, deliberately didn't smooth his clay (now translated into bronze), leaving it rough and choppy. It's as if Cardot took Churchill's voice, that obstinate, gruff intelligence of his, and created a body from it. I like to walk by and give the prime minister an imaginary salute.

I've arrived in Bochum, Germany, to give a talk about Renaissance London at the German Shakespeare Society conference. Alessandro will join me in a few days. The train from Paris to Cologne took me through farmland where clusters of delicate white windmills stood like storks, chattering together on a hilltop.

Before I got on the train, Alessandro assured me that everyone — but *everyone* — in Germany speaks English. This may be true in Berlin or Hamburg, but it is definitely not true in Bochum, a not-large city in North Rhine–Westphalia. In the first restaurant I wandered into with my friend Steven, another American professor, there was a panic when neither of us knew any German, nor did the staff in front speak English. At length the cook emerged from the kitchen in his apron and translated the menu for us. The next day, the same thing happened in a different restaurant: only the cook spoke English. Perhaps cooks are particularly adept at languages, or perhaps they are more nomadic than the average Bochum resident.

On Saturday I had a free morning, so I wandered around Bochum. The city was having a cultural festival, with stands lining the main streets. I was fascinated to see three stout and highly respectable German ladies of a certain age at a beer stand, gripping large steins. Mind you, it was only ten o'clock. My German colleagues later told me that the ladies were enjoying *Frühschoppen,* or an "early glass" — reserved for special occasions.

My hotel backs onto a park with a lovely lake. Yesterday I saw a cormorant at the very top of a tree, poised against the sky with his wings spread. I watched him for at least five minutes as he stayed there, motionless, drying his wings after a swoop into the water. He held his head high, as if he were meditating on something far more serious than the fish population of a lake in Bochum, Germany.

Alessandro arrived last night, and crossing the park near our hotel on the way to dinner, we walked straight into a bunny party. There must have been at least twenty of them fooling around, far too busy having fun to pay attention to us. I could not help thinking about the utter joy at the end of *The Velveteen Rabbit,* when the toy rabbit is made real because the Boy loved him so much, and he finds himself in the woods, in the moonlight, playing with real rabbits.

Our hotel here in Bochum has a little stand in the lobby called Struppi's Buffet, with food and drink for visiting dogs. Other things I love about this hotel: the bathroom lights turn on only if you put your room card in a slot. Electricity is saved, and I haven't misplaced my card once. What's more, in the shower you choose, via computer, the precise degree of warm water you'd like: no edging the knobs infinitesimally to the right or left, trying to achieve a tolerable temperature.

■ ■ ■ ■

I have been hearing fascinating stories about the reunification of East and West Germany from the point of view of German Shakespeareans. Before the fall of the Berlin Wall, in 1989, there were two Shakespeare societies in the two Germanys, with two presidents, two boards of directors, two essay collections, and two conferences. We academics care ferociously about our hierarchies — yet when the Wall fell, the two separate fiefdoms had to become one. These days, the reunited Shakespeareans have a cautiously sanguine air, like a couple who remarried after years of estrangement.

While I was listening to studious, thoughtful papers addressing Shakespeare's work, Alessandro tried out a swimming pool recommended by the hotel. On arrival he discovered that it was, in fact, a "textile-free" spa, a rather prudish description for a place designed for frolicking without clothing. The spa contained a dazzling number of saunas, over fifteen, each offering a different experience — the "Himalayan sauna," for example, followed by the "TV sauna." To my mind, the sheer number of saunas suggested erotic activity, but Alessandro strayed into the "Sahara" and found it already occupied by a respectable (if naked) middle-aged couple, who were merely sitting about and sweating together. The swimming pool was kidney-shaped and clearly meant for lounging rather than laps. He wandered about intrepidly, clutching his towel, but said later that it would have been more fun if I'd been there. Apparently everyone else was in pairs. In case you're wondering, I refused to make a visit.

On the train back to Paris, we found ourselves behind an American couple fighting viciously because, it emerged, he had made fun of her gait. (I would like to add in my defense that it was impossible not to eavesdrop, given the energetic way they conducted this conversation.) She was plump and miserable, and I felt for her, although her reliance on the F-word as noun, verb, and adjective was grating. They had been married three years, it seemed. Finally, she hissed, "You are not so important in my life," and left. And then I truly felt sorry for her, since she felt that way about the man she'd married. Alessandro *is* that important in my life. (Though, for the record, he wouldn't dream of making fun of the way I walk. He has a strong survival instinct.)

After yesterday's sad train experience, I've been thinking about marriage. There's no getting around the fact the institution leads to the best and the worst of times. The other day Alessandro looked at me and said, "Are you going out like that?" I briefly contemplated homicide. But then last night he squeezed me and said, "Don't lose weight. I like it when you're curvy." I was so glad I hadn't slain him.

Alessandro and I have discovered a wonderful shop: Heratchian Frères in rue Lamartine, which specializes in *produits alimentaires exotiques et d'Orient.* As in some epicure pirate's cave, there are shelves of mysterious cans; huge sacks of tiny orange lentils, barley, and cornmeal; knee-high containers of brined olives; and five kinds of feta. One section was all Turkish delight: rose-flavored, pistachio-flavored, *double* pistachio-flavored. A shelf glimmering in the corner proved to be crowded with jars containing seven different shapes of silver dragées, edible decorations that really do look like pirate booty.

We decided to pull Anna out of school for a

few days because the "centers for leisure" are open, and she seems to learn more French in a day of playing in one of them than in three months of French class. We entered the room to a scene of chaos, kids dashing in every direction. Anna held my hand tightly, and then a teacher strolled out, playing his guitar. They all ran to him, Pied Piper-style. "Anna!" he called with a grin, and her hand slipped from mine and she was off.

I took friends to the Musée Jacquemart-André today. This was my second visit, but before now I never noticed a gorgeous little porcelain *Rape of Ganymede* tucked in a deep alcove at the top of the grand staircase. Ganymede was the boy stolen by Zeus to become his cupbearer. As the most beautiful boy on earth, he's often depicted with lush sensuality; here, he's a slender, wistful youth, on the verge of leaving home.

Another discovery: the extraordinary Paolo Uccello, *Saint George and the Dragon,* in the Florentine Gallery. In the fifteenth-century panel, a princess — whom Saint George is in the process of rescuing — stands just behind the dragon, which has a perfectly corkscrewed tail. She is wearing a red velvet gown with pearls sewn in flower patterns, and orange slippers, but her finery is diminished by her pale, docile face and her attitude of prayer. She's making no attempt to run, and I couldn't help thinking that she's put a lot of faith in Saint George's untested reptile-slaying abilities. Luckily, Saint George is, in fact, adroitly skewering the dragon.

Across the street from our apartment is a little hotel, Hôtel Peyris Opéra, which Anna calls the Harry Potter hotel because of its initials. Paris is gloriously warm and spring-like, and today the hotel's restaurant put three little café tables out in front, with white tablecloths, rose-colored wineglasses, and pink flowers. I have to stay at my computer, but the only thing I want to do is put on a dress and some heels, go downstairs, and drink wine in the sunshine.

OF RICE AND MEN

Back in 1990, rice and love became forever entwined in my mind. A man I'd dated for ten years broke off our relationship, and my response to grief was to learn how to make risotto. A few months later, I went on a blind date with Alessandro, and some time after that found myself in Florence, seeking the approval of my future mother-in-law, whose favorite dish was risotto. Rice and love.

When my long-term relationship went awry, I was living in a tiny apartment in the graduate ghetto of New Haven, Connecticut. I spent my free time cooking, crying, and reading. My favorite cookbook was Paul Bertolli's *Chez Panisse Cooking,* a collection of fervent essays that included a long piece on risotto. I would stand over the pot, stirring as Paul instructed, reading a romance borrowed from the public library, and crying every now and then when it seemed the heroines had a better life than I did. After a month or two of this, I was quite good at risotto, and I started to think about men in a more cheerful manner, which led to a blind date with Alessandro, then a graduate student in Italian with loopy black curls and a swimmer's body. He invited me to his house for dinner. I wore a tiny black minidress with over-the-knee green suede boots. The evening was a success, so I reciprocated. He loved my risotto. It wasn't until years later, when I ate his mother's creamy, delicious risotto, that I understood how crucial that tiny detail was to our future life.

Risotto recipes are everywhere, though I do recommend reading Bertolli's book, if you can. The basic recipe has an onion, a little garlic, Arborio rice, a cup of white wine, and homemade broth. But this is a recipe that's like love: you must savor every step. When you can smell that the onions are soft but not brown, add the garlic. When you smell the garlic's burst of perfume, throw in the rice and stir until it takes on a glossy, plumpy sheen. The smell of wine should leap from the pan when you pour it in, and finally — Paul is right about this — the broth goes in slowly, ladle by ladle. Stir. These days, I listen to podcasts while I stir, rather than read romances, but it's all the same: a slow brewing pot, a stir, another stir.

Chez Panisse risotto came to me when I was heartbroken, and led straight to a risotto-adoring Italian with whom I fell in love and whom I married. And that led to his mother, with her wooden spoon and passion for broth, to my daughter, whose favorite food is risotto with roasted squash.

Luca's history teacher is very demanding, and he favors the Socratic method. Naturally, as soon as he announces that it is time for an *interrogazione,* the students all line up to go to the bathroom. From the refuge of the loo, Luca texted a friend — "Who's chosen?" — and got the texted reply "Just starting." Luca: "Is he done?" Silence. Luca couldn't stay in the bathroom forever, so he finally returned to find his poor friend miserably standing in front of the class.

"He's so *French,*" Alessandro said of Florent, upon returning home from conversation exchange today. "He goes on and on about Pauline: so passionate, so in love. But has he told her any of this? No." According to my husband, if Florent were Italian instead of French, he would already be booked into a honeymoon hotel. Remembering Alessandro's style of courtship, I would agree.

Last night the air was so warm and beautiful that Alessandro and I walked much farther than usual — all the way past would-be aristocrats enjoying champagne on the lawns of the Louvre, down through the Tuileries, toward the Opéra . . . at last collapsing into Café de la Paix, with its gaudy, gilded (but quite lovely) ceiling. My hot chocolate came in two silver pitchers. One held melted chocolate, as dark and thick as lava, the second steaming hot milk. Heaven!

On a Minnesota prairie, the night sky is lightened only by a bowl of stars. Sometimes, when I was growing up, we even caught a shimmer of the northern lights. Paris, on the other hand, is *never* dark. In our bedroom, peacock blue taffeta curtains start at the ceiling and puddle on the floor. But at night, light from the street creeps above the rod and bathes the room; it reminds me that I'm in a city, surrounded by people. And I love it.

The first of May is the French Labor Day,

which at home brings a parade. Here, it means a huge protest. People flooded into Paris, thousands of them. Each unit has its own music; I was proud that many labor groups were represented by American hip-hop. There were also live bands playing traditional French music, and some singing verses that seemed mostly to consist of rhymes such as "Sarkozy — *oui!*"

As well as protesting, on May Day Parisians buy lilies of the valley in twists of paper and give them to each other. Alessandro bought me a posy, and then an extraordinarily nice Frenchman gave me another on the street (a surprising and delightful moment), so now I have a glassful of little fairy bonnets in shy curls next to me, like a scrap of the deep forest on my desk. Apparently, in the language of flowers these lilies of the valley signal a return of happiness. I feel happier than I would if they were diamonds.

After extensive research, I have a blueprint for the perfect tart. It should be very small, hardly more than a bite, and have a buttery, flaky crust, a bit of pastry cream, and a miniature tower of raspberries. One or two berries should be topped with edible gold leaf, in order to create the illusion that the eater is Marie Antoinette herself, wearing a spun-sugar wig, nibbling cakes, and handing out dining advice.

Only after months of walking under gleaming gold statues of Pegasus, each paired with a different nymph waving a sword — that is, the four statues on Pont Alexandre III — have I noticed something very interesting. The horses have ferocious erections. I'm just saying.

I took Nicole and Anna to the Italian ice cream shop Amorino after school. A big placard outside lists the various sizes of servings offered. I wasn't paying attention and somehow allowed the girls to talk me into ordering two "grandissimo" cups. First of all, this was exorbitantly expensive. Second, it turned out to be more ice cream than I'd ever seen in a cup before. Rather cross with myself — and not pleased with them either — I told the girls that they had to eat it *all.* As they neared the end, I added the proviso that no one was allowed to vomit. Anna finished, but Nicole reluctantly admitted that the second provision outweighed the first, and handed over her grandissimo cup with a spoonful or two of ice cream left inside.

■ ■ ■ ■

For the third time, I walked through Musée Nissim de Camondo and listened to the audiotape (I could be a guide, by this point). This time I lingered in the dining room, looking at a bronze *Bust of a Negress,* from the early nineteenth century. Apparently it came from a grouping designed for a fountain in which a black servant woman, cast in dark bronze, poured water over her white mistress, carved from marble. There's a lot to think about there, and none of it very good.

In the afternoon I walked through a little park by place de la Concorde that is full of flowering horse chestnut trees, each prim white petal with a cherry-colored heart. There had been a windstorm. I kicked my way through drifts of blossoms, heaped and piled as if they were sawdust.

Here is an Anna refrain: "I hate fish, unless it's bass." This is because once upon a time, in a long-ago, halcyon summer, her brother caught a bass in a Minnesota lake, and she still remembers eating that fish with pleasure. Put it up to a mother's ingenuity: *every* fish I cook is a bass (no matter what the French fishmonger might care to call them).

We discovered a wonderful crêperie, Breizh Café, which makes classic Breton crepes from dark buckwheat flour. The menu is marvelously varied, from savory to sweet. I had a crepe made with bitter orange marmalade and Cointreau. Set aflame, naturally. We sat next to a grandfather and his eight-or nine-year-old grandson. They each had a huge classic crepe — with just a dusting of sugar. They ate them up, and then Grandpa summoned the waiter: two more of the same! They talked about lions, about how fast and fierce they are. I thought of a kindly grandpa lion, lying in the shade of a baobab tree, sharing bones and stories with a cub.

Math exams are still terrifying prospects for Luca. He has a tutor once a week, and many nights he and Alessandro work late, puzzling out his calculus homework. A few days ago he came home despondent; there had been a test, and while comparing answers with others after class, Luca discovered that no one had come up with the same numbers he did. But today the grades were handed out. Guess who got the second-best grade in the class?

My beloved father is losing his memory. Today I got a letter from him, with the correct street address but without my name, or indeed any name. Luckily, our mail carrier figured out that letters from the United States were probably for us. Inside, Dad enclosed a copy of his lovely poem, just published in *The New Yorker:* "I have daughters and I have sons." I am so afraid of the day when there are no more poems, or letters.

Luca's Italian literature class just finished reading Homer's *Iliad,* the ancient story of warriors storming the city of Troy. His friends have nicknamed one of their classmates Achilles because he's always angry and destructive; indeed, classroom chairs and tables have toppled before his wrath. Alessandro suddenly recalled a boy in his middle school class who'd been labeled Fast-Footed Achilles because of his speed. There's something to be said about the downfall of culture in these two examples. . . .

Last week I wrote about kicking my way

through drifts of flowers, and today I learned that Claude had the same experience. His flowers covered the ground like "white foam," and his eyes filled suddenly with tears in response to "the unfettered soul of beauty." I might have to stop reading his book. Claude's overblown rhetoric makes me feel both surly and superior, a bad combination. I suspect that my irritation stems not from his sentimentality but from the fact that he is indisputably my predecessor, if not my prototype: we are describing the same flowers, albeit one hundred years apart. I don't like to think of my great-niece chortling over my rhetoric, but I suspect it's inevitable.

FIGHTING THROUGH THE HOLIDAYS

All good Minnesotans head "up North" in July, landing alongside Canada geese at lakes crowded with speedboats and pasty-legged vacationers of Scandinavian descent. My clearest memory from my family's northerly adventures was the summer when my parents were splitting up. I can't bring to mind their actual fights (though I was dimly aware that finances and infidelity were pressing concerns); I wasn't paying attention. Who had time? I was sixteen, and obsessed with earning the money to buy myself a pair of white painter's pants with a little loop on the side, clearly designed for a teenage boy to hook his finger through. A deep tan would have been a cheaper route to "hot babe," but since my gene pool ruled that out, I had fixated on those pants as the key to landing a boyfriend. The effort required to keep this magical thinking afloat meant that I had no mental energy left with which to dissect my parents' surging, embarrassing emotions.

That summer my father was in charge of making lunch, which wasn't unusual; my mother embraced shared housework the moment Betty Friedan put pen to paper. But Dad's repertoire was not large: scrambled eggs, spaghetti, applesauce — and tongue. He specialized in big, boiled tongues. Because grocery shopping had broken down in the face of escalating hostilities, a hunk of tongue always seemed to be on the kitchen counter, labeled "lunch." I would stare at it, repulsed, until I became so hungry that I would douse a piece in salt and choke it down, my own tongue curling in an effort to avoid the pebbled texture. My sister, who was both more sensitive and more slender, skated near anorexia from pure tongue-loathing. My appetite was stronger than my revulsion; I did not lose a pound, but I did lose all respect for my parents.

Had anyone asked me at the time, I would have confidently asserted that I would never expose my future children to the revolting sights and sounds of marital strife. To our credit, Alessandro and I largely succeed in avoiding acrimony; steering clear of infidelity helps. Still, as they were for my parents, vacations are when we break into open warfare — and our flash point is money. To put it in a nutshell, I like a good splurge; my husband, on the other hand, can be frugal to a fault. Vacation puts such differences front and center.

Even before we decided to move to Paris, we had talked of a visit to the Loire Valley and its castles, and eventually we decided the trip should also celebrate Luca's sixteenth birthday. I was in charge of finding a suitable restaurant for the birthday dinner itself; Alessandro's mission was to find a hotel within driving distance of several castles. On a website boasting cheap deals, he found a hotel offering a suite, with a living room and kitchen, at an amazing rate. Because the hotel was brand-new, it hadn't been reviewed. That was a bit worrisome, but the price was low enough to overcome such fiddling fears.

By this point in the book, you may have deduced that I have a weakness for luxury. When it comes to hotels, sheets with thread counts higher than the national debt make me happy, as do little bottles of shampoo, particularly if labeled in the imperative: "Nourish," for example. Or "Enhance." From our first glimpse of the Cheapskate Hotel, I realized there would be no such civilizing treats. The rental car's GPS disclaimed knowledge of the address, but somehow we chanced on an unpaved road running around an industrial complex, ending at a construction site on which a naked concrete building rose from the dust. Voilà. Our hotel.

Having checked in at a linoleum-covered counter, we were directed to a room on the fourth floor, where we emerged from the elevator to discover — the hard way — that the corridors were illuminated by motion-detector lights on a slight delay. Standing in the pitch dark, we froze until fluorescent tubes spasmed on, revealing dispiriting gray industrial carpeting — whose color continued straight into the rooms. Not that the color of our suite's carpet was much in evidence: the previous occupants had thrown quite a party, judging by the dirty dishes, the pyramid of empty wine bottles, and the way cigarette ashes sprinkled the carpeting like dandruff on a church warden.

Downstairs, the manager threw up his hands and sent us to another suite, this one on the third floor. We opened the door to a room that had apparently been shared by about three dozen backpackers, if the sand dune–size debris pile left behind was any indication. By this point I had moved from dismay to open revolt, and headed back downstairs prepared to make a break for freedom and a hotel with three stars — or even *one*. And then came the moment of truth: Alessandro confessed that he had prepaid the entire week. "Third time lucky!" he said, trying for a jaunty air. But he came off sounding like a flight attendant offering a second bag of pretzels during a five-hour tarmac delay. In response my face took on the snarl of a saber-toothed tiger. While this is a look those long-suffering flight attendants are probably used to, my children were not.

Will it surprise you to learn that the third time was *not* lucky? This time we schlepped our bags to the second floor, where the kitchen sink turned out to be free from dirty dishes. But we hardly noticed, too riveted by the smoke-blackened windows, intricately crazed in cobwebby patterns. It seemed that the hotel backed onto train tracks (which, as we learned later, handled an active timetable), and there had been a fire under the railroad bridge. One might surmise that the fire originated in the ramshackle shantytown under the bridge, but such speculation was irrelevant. We had identified the tenor of the neighborhood just by checking in.

"If I push this," Anna observed, running a finger over the crazed glass, "the window kind of bulges out. See? Isn't that cool?"

My heart was beating in a way that suggested an imminent stroke, so I retreated into the master bedroom. The bed bore a concave impression, perhaps of a person who had relaxed there to watch television while she should have been cleaning other rooms, and who was kind enough to have left the TV on so that guests could enjoy it. By that point, I wanted nothing more than to charge back into the living room and scream insults at my spouse while throwing my suitcase through that disintegrating window. But the ghost of my sixteen-year-old self stood at my shoulder, whispering, "Not in front of the children." I gritted my teeth, lay down, and watched TV — which, of course, was in French, so I didn't understand a thing. At that point, I couldn't have imagined that things could get worse.

But the day was not over.

I had made reservations for Luca's birthday dinner at a charming country restaurant, acclaimed for its traditional cuisine. Accordingly, we bundled the children into their best clothes — even though getting a teenage boy into a button-down shirt practically takes an act of Parliament — and took

252

off. Yes, there was some tension in the car during the drive there. Luca was brooding over the indignity of my sartorial choices, and Alessandro had taken umbrage at my dislike of the hotel. But I practiced taking deep breaths and calling on the Zen side of myself that I'd always meant to cultivate. No time like the present!

The restaurant's exterior was hung with ivy and flowers; inside it was all hushed white tablecloths and bowing waiters, and a big sign specifying NO CELL PHONES in several languages. We were ushered to our table by a very, very *French* waiter.

I suspect most people grapple with a prejudice of one kind or another. Given how they beam while announcing that they would *never* have guessed I was American, I rather think a lot of French people have zeroed in on my countrymen as the objects of their contempt. As for me? I have, over the course of my life, developed a deep intolerance for the archetypal French waiter: a supercilious, sanctimonious, self-important man in black. I particularly loathe the way such men intimidate their customers into a state of cowed gratitude, from which submissive posture the customers beg for advice — which is invariably delivered with a barely concealed Gallic sneer.

Alessandro now embarked on just such a conversation with our waiter, about champagne. We had decided that a sixteenth birthday should be celebrated with a toast, but because I am wary about children drinking alcohol (a notion both Italians and French ridicule), I had stipulated mimosas. As our fluent family representative, Alessandro was thus forced to explain the concept of a mimosa to our ever-more-haughty waiter.

It hardly need be said that Monsieur did little to contain his distaste at the idea of pouring *juice* into *wine.* I felt defensive, judged, and outclassed; even Alessandro grew flustered. At that point his cellphone rang. Monsieur's brow darkened, but Alessandro flipped the phone open and then proceeded to punch the wrong button, putting it in speaker mode at precisely the moment a group of Italian relatives gathered together to scream *"Buon compleanno"* to Luca. A second later they began singing their birthday greetings.

"Close the phone!" I snapped at Alessandro.

"I can't!" he hissed back. "It's my *mother.*"

I was now in the throes of deep humiliation. Sedate, decorous couples all around us turned their heads in our direction. To judge by the clamor emitting from the phone, Marina was handing the cellphone around on her end, and a whole tableful of Italians were taking turns shrieking their best wishes to Luca. At this point, Alessandro looked up at the waiter's glittering black eyes and asked — humbly — "Would it be all right with you if we ordered glasses of champagne for the children?"

Confirmed in his conviction that he was master of the universe, Monsieur stalked away, shoulders tight with scorn, and returned with four large bell-shaped glasses of champagne. Then, with a withering flourish, he put down two unopened bottles of orange juice.

We managed to place our orders, but by then my sixteen-year-old ghost was long forgotten, and I had lost both my control and my self-respect. It wasn't until Alessandro ventured the opinion that I had better look out or I would turn into my mother that I decided it was time to remove ourselves from our children's presence.

"But where are you going?" Anna demanded.

"Tell the waiter we've gone to smoke a cigarette," Alessandro replied.

"You don't smoke," she wailed.

Some moments should be relived only between spouses, so I will draw a discreet curtain over the wretched way we screamed at each other in the quiet cobblestone street. By the time we returned to the table — pretty much reconciled to marital existence — our entrées had arrived, and the champagne was gone. Luca, the guest of honor, sat stone-faced, in the grip of an adolescent disgust that I instantly recognized. His face threw me straight back to the summer of the painter's pants, the boiled tongue, the impending divorce. Meanwhile, Anna had taken advantage of our absence to gulp not only her own champagne but ours as well. She was giggling madly, an empty walnut shell balanced on top of her head. The walnut was serving as a witch's hat, and she had been amusing herself by acting out the Harry Potter characters one after another for the benefit of her mortified brother. (Have I mentioned this was an elegant, and very dignified, restaurant?)

Early on in our year in France, I had resolved to eat adventurously while here, and in that spirit I had ordered a local delicacy: *tête de veau.* Calf's head. Now I saw that the *tête* had been transformed into a little pie — over which was draped a limp, ruddy-colored rooster's comb. Monsieur le Waiter reappeared and explained that a boiled cockscomb was the perfect accompaniment to a pie made of brains, and that they should be eaten together. At this point Luca abandoned his silent protest and made his first contribution to his sixteenth-birthday party: an exaggerated retching noise.

I didn't even look up to see what the other guests or the waiter made of my children's behavior. I was too transfixed by the boiled rooster comb.

My father's penchant for boiled tongue — as well as my mother's wrath over lavish purchases that the family could not afford — came back to me in a rush.

In one day, I had reproduced an entire summer from my childhood.

The rooster comb brought back the deep despair that reverberated through our family that July — the way no grown-ups noticed that my sister had virtually stopped eating, and the way no grown-ups ever spoke to each other quietly, let alone civilly. Alessandro and I, on the other hand? We could sleep on thousand-thread-count sheets or sheets that felt like grain-sack burlap, and we would still be talking to each other the next morning. We will always notice if one of our children stops eating. We have learned not to hold grudges over Cheapskate Hotels and snide French waiters.

The rooster comb was quite good, in its own way.

The brain pie? Inedible.

Château de Blois was the scene of the Duke of Guise's murder in 1588 by King Henri III, and there's a truly creepy feeling knowing that the bedchamber was, as Henry James put it, "the scene of the principal events of [Henri III's] depraved and dramatic reign." Children being the depraved and dramatic creatures they are, Anna and Luca fought to stand on the exact spot where Guise was stabbed by eight assailants.

After our visit to the Blois castle, Anna and I decided that the scariest gargoyles aren't lizardlike or dragonlike, with scales and tails and pointed ears. No, the human gargoyles are far more terrifying, with their blank eyes and toothless, open mouths. They look like the souls Dante describes in the *Inferno,* mouths stretched open in an eternal howl.

In the main square of the town of Blois is a Maison de la Magie — i.e., a magic museum. Six golden dragon heads emerge from windows on the upper story of the museum and roar into the plaza. They have long, wicked snouts and pale blue eyes that seem all the more ferocious for being such a limpid color.

My favorite place in Orléans is the Chocolaterie Royale, where we bought chocolate oranges, almond bark, white chocolate cranberry bark, and — the best — chocolate medallions featuring the Joan of Arc statue in the main square. Feeling guilty over the hotel debacle, Alessandro kept bringing more to the counter until we had spent approximately half the price of our hotel room on an artisanal-chocolate bender.

For someone like Anna — who spends her days (a) reading Harry Potter books, and (b) examining her hair to see if it curls like Hermione's yet, and (c) trying to find a stick that might be a magic wand — a jaunt around French castles is like a repeat visit to Disneyland. She squealed at Chambord's great hall (just like Hogwarts!), greeted the Blois suit of armor (in Hogwarts, suits of armor are quite chatty), and became joyously lost in the maze at Château de Chenonceaux (alas, no magic cup to be

259

found).

The Château de Chenonceaux was the site of great jockeying between Catherine de' Medici, queen to Henri II, and Henri's mistress, Diane de Poitiers, to whom he gave the castle. When Henri died, Catherine took it back. Diane had had a portrait of herself painted in which she was depicted as the goddess Diana, so Catherine did the same — and the two portraits now hang together in one of the salons. Diane makes the more delectable Diana.

Beatrice adroitly holds her place as the Queen Bee of the fourth grade by arbitrarily dismissing some girls and then welcoming others (though never Anna). Today she summarily jettisoned a classmate named Maria from the cool group, for reasons known only to Her Majesty. "Maria cried all day," Anna told me. "I felt bad for her, but she thinks I'm weird, so I couldn't help."

My friend Anne and I explored the tiny Musée Bourdelle today. Antoine Bourdelle (1861–1929) was a sculptor; the museum was his house and atelier. In the garden, I fell in love with *Le Fruit,* a statue of Eve with a luscious little smirk and a sinuous twist to her hips. In her right hand, three apples. In her left, behind her back, another apple. Woven into her hair . . . apples! And then upstairs we found an exquisite *Bacchante,* one of Bacchus's female groupies — a wilder version of Eve, with the same sexy twist to her hips, but ivy in her hair instead of apples.

Luca says that the fact that Alessandro and I launched into a battle during his sixteenth-birthday celebration has undoubtedly scarred him forever and he will never go on vacation with us again. In the meantime, he would like his computer back so that he can communicate with other teens whose parents are raving nuts. We are united in our decision that he will have to survive without the tender support of his peers until he passes ninth grade.

Today I made great headway in Claude's book, as Alessandro kept me waiting in a café and I had it with me. Claude held forth on the "unconscious grace of movement, the gentleness of manner, the instinctive courtesy" that characterizes the upper classes. He says that aristocracy lingers "like a perfume above bare existence." I'm afraid my response was rather hostile. *You were born in Duluth, Minnesota, Claude. Just who do you think you are kidding?*

Last night Alessandro and I walked home as the sky turned periwinkle blue, on the cusp of twilight. At the end of rue du Conservatoire is La Pause, a tiny bar where music students hang out at the end of the day. Two men sat outside playing guitars; one of them started whistling, and the clear, twinkling music followed us down the street, filling the air all the way up to that darkening sky.

I've become obsessed with tracking down a song I heard in a store, a French version of Bob Dylan's "Blowin' in the Wind." It turns out there are many covers; the one I was chasing was Richard Anthony's 1964 *"Écoute dans le vent."* (Despite his Anglo name, he's an Egyptian-born Frenchman.) In the video I found online, he stands in a black sweater, his hands nonchalantly pushed into his pockets, and sings while behind him musicians in narrow-lapelled suits and ties strum their guitars. In 1963 and '64, Dylan belted out that song as a protest against the American idea of manhood and its celebration of violence and war; he was singing at a time when our military involvement in Vietnam was escalating rapidly. Much as I love Anthony's version, he turned a protest song into supper-club music . . . it makes you wonder if he even understood the lyrics.

Today we actually bid on a painting at Hôtel Drouot, though we didn't win. It was a gorgeous little seventeenth-century Madonna. Following the directions of more experienced friends, we had determined an upper price. But someone else, behind us, wanted our Madonna. He bid; Alessandro bid. Up and up it went, until we reached our limit. Alessandro looked at me and hesitated. The auctioneer helpfully jumped in: "Madame says yes!" We laughed and went higher, until Alessandro gave me another nervous look, and I shook my head. "Monsieur," the auctioneer said as we stood up to leave, "we have more paintings that Madame will say yes to!" But we avoided the siren call of winning for the sake of it and went to lunch instead.

Today I went to Le Phare de la Baleine, which translates into the Whale's Lighthouse, a store where locals buy those fabulous striped T-shirts — the authentic version, not the ones for tourists. They also have adorable children's clothing, and thick beach towels, cherry-colored and sprinkled with little white whales. I bought a fabulous pale blue straw hat, shaped with four square points and a bow. Now I'm home, I think the bow is rather twee, though perhaps on a French madame it looks retro and ironic.

When I arrived at college, straight from a Minnesota farm, I was terrified by the kids in cashmere and linen who had spent their holidays skiing in the Alps. The memory of those boys — "euros," we called them, long before that word defined a continent's currency — remained repressed until yesterday, when I took Luca shopping. He picked out three things in five minutes: dark red jeans, a crinkly pink T-shirt, and a torso-hugging, finely knit sweater. He now looks precisely like the boys who petrified and intimidated me . . . because he *is* one. I have given birth to the enemy.

I have developed a fail-safe way to cook fish with skin: you first cut a crisscross pattern in the skin. Then you rub the flesh with a seasoning mixture containing at least a hint of curry (Galeries Lafayette has a freshly ground mixture labeled "couscous"). Heat some olive oil over a high flame and sauté the fish skin side down (if it's a whole fish, turn it once). When it's browned, pour lemon juice over it and pop it in the oven for five minutes if it's not already white and flaky. This will give you a crisp, crackling skin and a faintly exotic flavor that even children will enjoy.

I'm sitting at my desk, just before seven in the morning. The sky outside my study window is a kind of pearl blue, so pale that it looks like the shadow of blue, or the memory of blue. Swallows are swooping over the rooftops across from me, flashing black across the sky and disappearing again.

I am having a new experience with the book I'm writing, a Regency version of *Beauty and the Beast*. Ordinarily I slave over my characters' lines, endlessly rewriting them. But this book is different. It's as if I were describing a movie happening right before me, which makes me feel oddly delirious.

Months in Paris have done nothing for my appalling French. This Sunday in church I was singing along merrily, half-thinking about the words. So nice, I thought, here we are singing that Jesus freed the fish: *"nous libérant du péché."* . . . No, no, that can't be right. Maybe it's a union song and Jesus freed the fishermen. Alessandro informs me that Seigneur Jésus freed us from sin. Sins, not sardines.

Florent and Pauline have finally broached the subject of romance with each other. Alas, when he laid his heart at her feet, she replied that she wasn't ready for a long-term commitment. He replied that she was like a lemon tart that he could see in a window but couldn't eat. He won my heart with that metaphor — though Alessandro pointed out (again) that if Florent were Italian, he would be in the patisserie and picking up the tart already.

It's getting warmer in France, and Parisian women have broken out their shorts. They go to work in the morning wearing tight knee-length shorts, often cuffed (and sometimes even in denim). These are combined with dignified jackets and high, high heels. The result is — rather to my surprise — stylish rather than skanky.

I have finished my version of *Beauty and the Beast!* To celebrate, we went out to our local Thai restaurant and discussed titles. Because my hero was inspired by the television program *House M.D.,* the kids are championing "The Cranky Cripple and the Bodacious Bride," but my editor tossed that for *When Beauty Tamed the Beast.* I like it, though I'm secretly afraid that my hero remains untamed as ever.

I was sitting at a café when an adorable two-year-old toddled past, wearing black tights, a black-and-white checked dress, and a black sweater. And a black barrette. No wonder Parisians are effortlessly sophisticated — they learn the virtues of a little black dress when we're all still wearing Disney T-shirts emblazoned with pink rhinestones and sunglasses to match.

I always jog down rue La Fayette, so that I can stop in front of Graziella, a minuscule store with two or three garments at most in its window. Everything they design and sell is striking, with flair and drama. The pieces, especially a coat with a flared collar and fabulous buttons, bring to mind an old Katharine Hepburn movie.

We are sending Luca and Anna to Italian tennis camp. Luca will follow that up with two more weeks of French tennis camp. He's furious about our social planning.

Given his druthers, he would sleep all day and be on Facebook (or worse) all night. But we retain sovereignty, for a little while longer.

THE HORROR THAT IS THE SCHOOL PLAY

My mother often said that her life ambitions were to marry a poet and become a ballet dancer. I have to suppose it was thwarted ambition that led to my sister and me being given dancing lessons. I have one memory, mercifully dim, of performing in a school play. I was an autumn leaf, prancing across the elementary school cafeteria with brown crinkly paper bobbing at my waist. I felt lumpish and decidedly unleaflike, and I was dismally aware that a gift for dancing hadn't emerged in my gene pool.

My children have inherited my regrettable genes: we're the spear carriers of school productions, ready to swell a chorus or play an attendant lord, or even, if needed, the Fool — but nothing more ambitious. This year, for the Italian school's production in French, Anna did not even achieve the level of the Fool. Luckily, her aspirations are commensurate with her thespian talents, so she was unperturbed when assigned the roles of a clock and a fly.

On the morning of the performance, she dressed all in black, as befits a fly. The only black T-shirt she has is emblazoned with the Ramones, so we instructed her to turn it inside out before going onstage, to ensure that the audience wouldn't think she was a punk insect. Her speaking responsibilities were small, but she did have to announce the time twice — in French, as she pointed out in a last-minute fit of nerves. *Tic-tac!*

On the way to school I asked her what the play was about, but she didn't seem to really know. She told me, rather uncertainly, that there was an old woman who died. It sounded like a Grimms' fairy tale to me. Wasn't there an old woman who ate a fly and died? But Anna assured me that she wasn't eaten.

That afternoon Alessandro and I arrived early for the performance and found Anna buzzing around the gym in her black outfit, now rounded out by a purple beak. This seemed remarkably unlike the flies I have known, and on inquiry it turned out that she'd mistaken her role — she wasn't a fly after all, but a little devil who buzzes around the dying woman as part of a bad dream. The plot was starting to sound oddly grim, even Kafkaesque. We settled in our seats to enjoy Dora the Dead as opposed to Dora the Explorer.

The ten-year-old "old lady" was recognizable front and center, wrapped in a blanket. But that was the last thing we understood. For one thing, Italian children babbling in French are none too intelligible. For another, the plot was made yet more obscure by the children's creative interpretations of their roles. A rather disaffected young girl, for example, kept taking long drafts from an (empty) wine bottle. I never figured out what her relationship to the dying woman was, or why she was courting inebriation, although Anna later informed me she was the narrator.

The plot grew even murkier as the inevitable technical glitches occurred. The mechanism drawing the curtain got stuck and started banging. The actors glanced upward and nervously continued jabbering in a way that suggested they comprehended about 50 percent of their lines, and really didn't mind if we in the audience comprehended zero. Devils came and went, dancing angels appeared, the clock's alarm went off (we enjoyed that), the drunk strode around the stage muttering. The audience began to have fits of laughter at inappropriate moments, which rattled the already perplexed actors.

The performance was slowly moving toward Anna's big moment — the clock's declaration of the time — when the "old lady" suddenly up and died. The other performers seemed rather surprised, but they gamely gathered around as she threw off her blanket and danced, in a rhythmic interpretation of heaven.

It turned out that the actress had grown befuddled and died two acts too soon. But by the time her error was recognized, it was beyond salvation. There was a general feeling (especially in the audience) that once the main character is dead, the play is over. It's time to draw the final curtain.

Anna never did get to say her big line, so she announced it at dinner instead. *"Il est neuf heures."* She said it very well.

The students in Florent's middle school have started calling Pauline Madame Selig (his last name), because the two of them spend so much time together. This is an interesting development. Teenagers are wickedly astute observers of adults; they perceive these two as a couple already. Now only Pauline needs convincing.

■ ■ ■ ■

Alessandro and I deserted the children for the evening and took ourselves out for dinner at a tiny new restaurant called Saveurs & Coïncidences. Our waitress was married to the chef; she told us that her husband had long dreamed of opening a restaurant where the food was so fresh that they had no need of a refrigerator. Some of the dishes were good and some were only so-so (Italian men — not to mention names — should just stop ordering risotto in other countries, because it *never* measures up), but the passion was unmistakable. And while Madame talked, a little boy in an appropriately sized chef's apron poked his head out of the kitchen.

We went to a big sports store today to buy many white garments for the children to wear at camp. Anna used her painfully saved allowance to buy a hot pink spelunking lamp that straps to her forehead. "For reading Harry Potter books under the covers," she told me. Someday, just maybe, she'll learn not to alert the policeman before she commits a crime.

■ ■ ■ ■

Today I went online to try to rootle out some facts about Claude. *Pages from the Book of Paris* was his first book; after that he wrote novels and more nonfiction, including something entitled *Opinions,* which has — enticingly — chapters entitled "Pornography" and "Meditations on Woman." I shudder to imagine what Claude thought of pornography, not to mention what he would have made of my novels. But I also found a review in which his Paris memoir was damned with faint praise for its "racy sketches." My mother never liked my romances, which she labeled "that sex stuff." Yet obviously my ignominious talent for "racy sketches" is hereditary — and stems from her side of the family!

Today we went to a fun, tiny museum, the Musée de la Vie Romantique, housing furniture and keepsakes that belonged to the writer George Sand. Frankly, the art isn't noteworthy, though the reconstruction of her drawing room is fascinating and made the visit worthwhile. That, and sitting down for a cup of tea in the little tearoom in the garden. A lush flowering vine with orange-red flowers hung over a brick wall at our backs, as if Nature herself were taunting the artists whose work she'd outdone.

Florent told Alessandro about a terrific Vietnamese restaurant called Minh Chau, so we went there for dinner last night. Ten tables barely fit into the space, and the food comes from the floor above, down a steep winding stair. It's shabby, decorated with plastic flowers, and a bit claustrophobic — but the food! I had an amazing carrot and coriander salad to start, delicately seasoned and scrumptious, followed by chicken with ginger so good that we almost licked the plates. The bill? The equivalent of fifteen dollars!

Alessandro went to Austria to give a talk at a university there and brought me back a box of bonbons, with Mozart's face on each one and marzipan cake inside. I asked, "These are good for my diet, right?" The professor assured me that they're calorie-free, and who am I to argue?

I was crossing my favorite bridge, Pont Alexandre III, this morning, and paused to say hello to the statue of the laughing merboy. Two tourists passed me, both holding small video recorders in front of their faces. They turned the cameras this way and that, desperate to record everything, as if documentation was somehow meaningful in itself. I want to *experience* where I am and what I'm seeing, not view it only through the eye of a camera, for canned viewing later.

Florent came to dinner again and told me that Pauline is extremely beautiful, very intelligent, and fascinating to talk to. She's twenty-six, which doesn't sound too young to me for a long-term relationship. Florent certainly looks much younger than forty-one; I originally assumed he was around thirty. He has such a delightful, shy French charm. I wish he would immigrate to the United States and marry one of my friends. We could serve lemon tarts at the wedding.

On our evening walks, Alessandro and I generally wander down my favorite shopping street, rue des Martyrs, passing Autour du Saumon — a shop that sells nothing but salmon. Yesterday we went in and had a serious conversation about six or seven types of smoked salmon before selecting one. We gobbled it up (delicious!), but I have never met a smoked salmon I didn't like, so perhaps all that deliberative, oh-so-French decision making was wasted on us.

The end of the school year is here, and I gather that Florent's middle school colleagues will have a long meeting and then, as per local custom, a much longer dinner, before they all disperse for the holidays. Alessandro doled out more Italian romantic advice, emphasizing direct physical action. Florent and his beloved have done nothing but talk for hours every time they meet; Alessandro thinks it's time to move to kissing. "Love is not made of words," he told me. A very male point of view.

It is Anna's last day of school, and I will walk home, down rue des Invalides, over Pont Alexandre III, say goodbye to the laughing mer-boy and Mr. Churchill, at least for now, walk through the lovely park by Concorde . . . Sweet "last times" pile up in my mind: the last time I hugged my mother, the last time I dried Luca off after a bath (now he towers over me), the last time I read aloud *Goodnight Moon* . . . I am still reading aloud to Anna, because I can't bear to think of the last book.

The final school assembly, held before all

parents, was a harrowing occasion. Paralyzed by nerves, Anna got stuck halfway through reading her story aloud and burst into tears. Domitilla jumped up to give her a long hug and then, as if tears were catching, burst into inconsolable tears herself because Anna was leaving Paris. How things have changed since last fall, when Domitilla was Enemy Number One!

Last night a little half block near us held a street party, with a band specializing in American hits from the seventies and eighties. We kept our bedroom windows open, the better to enjoy the free concert. One song that will forever remain in my memory is their rendition, with strong French accents, of "Play that funky music, white boy. Wew — hewwww!" We were hysterical with laughter. At some point, Luca burst into the room howling: "Listen! They're trying the White Stripes now!"

Viviane invited us over for dinner last night. The meal began with her rendition of an appetizer she'd recently eaten at a three-star Michelin restaurant (to die for) and ended with a cake that she bought from "the best patisserie in Paris" — Dalloyau on boulevard Beaumarchais. The inside was in various layers: a tart raspberry mousse, topped with a delicate lemon layer, surrounded by pistachio sponge cake with a gorgeous stenciled pattern in raspberry sugar. The top was glossy with a pale lemon sheen and held a delicate arrangement of berries. The next day we marched to that patisserie, bought the same cake, and took it home to devour.

The one thing that has cast a pall on my happiness here has been my hair; it's truly been the Year of Bad Hair. First I was given bright gold highlights, then a young lady troweled on platinum blond dye. The disapproving hairdresser who followed that disaster managed to create one of her own, turning me a garish orange with vegetable dye. Now that dye has faded, except near the scalp, where I am still carroty. Desperate searching online has revealed an English-speaking salon, StylePixie. Their website announces, "For hair emergencies please call the salon." I called the salon.

Musée Carnavalet is the museum of the history of the city of Paris, and that means everything plus the kitchen sink is thrown into its nearly one hundred rooms. They are mostly historically authentic rooms, removed from their original sites and re-installed here: Louis XVI's *salon bleu,* Marie Antoinette's drawing room, Marcel Proust's bedroom. Given the choice, I have to admit, I'd choose gawking at famous people's bedrooms over great art every time (the sign of a superficial mind, obviously).

Huzzah! Florent's end-of-school dinner wore on into the night . . . eating, drinking, smoking, celebrating. In the end, he and Pauline left the restaurant together and walked around the city. They wandered from the Bastille down rue du Faubourg-Saint-Antoine, then turned up boulevard Voltaire to République, talking madly, walking until dawn. Finally, when the sun was just pink over the Seine, Pauline looked at him and said, "You compared me to a lemon tart that you could not eat." He nodded. She opened her bag, and nestled in the bottom was a perfect little lemon tart.

A SLICE OF PARISIAN SUMMER

This morning I saw the family off to Italy; for the next two weeks, Alessandro will stay in Italy while the children are in tennis camp. I am remaining in Paris to write, write, write. As I reentered the apartment, it came to me that I've never been the one left behind; generally I'm the one who travels. Silence swelled in the apartment until it drummed in my ears. But now rain is pouring down the windows, and soon I will take my polka-dot umbrella out for a walk through city streets. Silence, with rain, is a friendly sound.

StylePixie Salon turned out to be the answer to my prayers. From the moment I entered and spotted a heap of U.K. women's magazines, I was happy. And after Victoria, the owner, assessed the ghastly situation on my head and delicately put in two or three different shades so as to tone down the orange and mask the platinum, I was in heaven.

The homeless man is gone. He packed up his tent and whisked himself away in the night. I hope he has found his way to somewhere green; I would like to think of him meditating on grass rather than concrete. I paused where his tent used to be and realized that it had been positioned on top of a powerful heating vent. No wonder he looked so comfortable, even in the depth of winter.

I'm writing a book about small theaters in London during Shakespeare's time, and I came across this lovely reference: in 1555, a quite powerful man named Sir Thomas Cawarden, who owned much of the fashionable area of London called the Blackfriars, wrote a lease agreement for one Elizabeth Foster. The lease gave her lodging "for the terms of her lyffe by the yearly rente of 3 odoriferus Flowers." By comparison, other people were paying upwards of thirty pounds a year, a huge amount at the time. The romance-writer part of me finds this contract both intriguing and agreeable.

I went to visit a friend in the 16th arrondissement today. She walked me back to the Métro stop, Porte Dauphine, and pointed out a glass canopy over the entrance that looks like a large, colorless peacock tail. Apparently, it is one of the few original Art Nouveau entrances left in the city. All that transparent glass arcing above the door seemed almost confrontational, as if to assert that this is *not* the door to the Underworld; Cerberus does not wait beneath.

Grades posted! We were afraid Luca might be remanded into the two-week remedial courses doled out to those with low grades. But no! He has worked incredibly hard this year to master Latin-into-Italian translations, geometry explained in Italian, and *interrogazioni* in history (routine complaint from teacher: "your facts are right, but your sentences aren't complicated enough"). Not only did he pass but he did very well indeed in some subjects! He appears to have a real gift for literary analysis (ahem).

I woke to silence and took myself out for a jog. Paris is moody, cool, and empty early in the morning. On my way home I found fruit sellers arranging artful mountains of apples, kiwis, and pineapples, like anxious (but artistic) squirrels stacking nuts for a long winter.

■ ■ ■ ■

I finished Claude's memoir, which concludes with a rather awkward imaginary interview with the writer Anatole France. The parallels between my great-uncle and me are remarkable. We both went to Harvard (I must give a nod to the tradition of legacy admissions here), moved to Paris, wrote memoirs, got emotional about French light, and wrote novels that were not admired by the literary establishment. Not only that, but we both wrote opinion pieces for *The New York Times*, though his was on Italian politics and mine was on the term *bodice-ripper*. And we did all of this almost precisely one hundred years apart. I called up Alessandro in Italy to inform him that I might be possessed by the ghost of Claude C. Washburn, but he merely snorted.

Milo is going on a thinning cure! Alessandro will be in the mountains while the children are in camp, and he's talked Marina into letting him take Milo with him. Marina packed Milo's red velvet pillow, his special dishes, his special coat, his special towel, and his special blow-dryer, and sent them off, admonishing Alessandro to keep him dry because the veterinarian says he is very, very sensitive and may get rheumatism if he's not coddled.

I spent yesterday at my computer, occasionally reaching over and savoring pieces of the chocolate shoe that Alessandro and Luca gave me: a touch of vanilla, an undertone of cocoa, a moody aftertaste. Silence, no cross teenager or needy eleven-year-old – – and a whole shoe to eat!

I just spoke to Anna, who called from camp. She told me, in a tone of pious virtue, "All the kids say swear words in every sentence. I can't tell you anything else because it would be tattling." Then, without pause, she added: "You know what Luca's doing? He's teaching his group American swear words — the really, really bad ones!" That's my boy . . . taking every opportunity to convey the finest aspects of American culture to his peers around the world.

Yesterday I encountered a line in front of a store selling British clothing — at 75 percent off. Naturally, I joined it. At the door I was handed a huge bag; inside, people were stuffing their bags with garments like ravenous pigeons scurrying after crumbs. In the end, I couldn't face the checkout line, and besides, I had lost a skirmish over a pale pink trench coat to a feral French woman. I slunk away, offering a weak smile to women still waiting in line outside.

Today Luca called from camp. His group has five sixteen-year-old boys and not a single girl his age; the oldest girl is thirteen. Six more campers arrive tomorrow: five boys and one more girl; he hopes fifteen or sixteen years old. "I'm the tallest," Luca told me, "and I score more than anyone at handball." Despite these potent factors, I gather he is unsure of winning The Girl. I just hope she's actually interested in boys.

After much sniffing, I have decided on my favorite French soap. It's made by a company called Resonances, and sold at Galeries Lafayette Maison in big blocks that you cut in half. It's scented with vervain, which I had to look up; it's a wildflower also called "herb of grace." The scent reminds me of lemons and wind-dried laundry.

I've been longing to check out the consignment-clothes scene in Paris, so I made my way to Réciproque, which has separate stores for men, women's evening clothes, women's designer clothes, and gift items. I tried on several Dior suits (all too expensive, but fun to wear, if momentarily), and then I decided I could afford a pale blue flowered Dior silk shirt. Hanging in my closet, it looks like a peacock among molting chickens.

Walking through the 7th arrondissement this morning, I looked up to see the Eiffel Tower at the end of the street. The city was so foggy that clouds completely obscured the tower's lower half; what was visible above the haze looked like the turret of a complicated, very dangerous submarine, emerging from a foggy sea. In fact, when the Eiffel Tower was erected, in 1889, there were widespread worries that it would alter the weather, and bring thunderstorms to the city. I suddenly understand the fear.

On French Women, and Whether They Get Fat

I came to Paris knowing I had one built-in friend waiting for me: a brilliant, funny banker named Sylvie, who happens to like reading my books in English. Long before we met in person, she used to write me and correct my defective French. Finally, I realized that I could spare myself further embarrassment by begging her to fix the French bits before publication. That changed the author-reader equation; we traded pictures of our children and stories of our marriages. Throughout the year she and I have met occasionally for lunch or dinner, during which I would bombard her with questions about French life. "No, we are *not* all adulterous!" she squealed at me once. Then: "Well, not in the suburbs, anyway." (She lives in the suburbs, I hasten to add.)

One day we decided to go shopping together — a casual decision that led me to a whole new philosophy about shopping and, beyond that, about dressing. When I'm in a store, I grab a skirt off the rack, hold it up to my waist, and jam it back in place. Sylvie, by contrast, moved thoughtfully here and there, touching the clothes delicately, as if they might fall to pieces. I took an armful of clothing into the dressing cabinet; she took one suit. When I finally emerged — having rejected the whole stack and put my own clothes on again — she was still in an adjacent mirrored room, conducting a lively forum with a number of store clerks as well as a few other customers.

To my eyes, the suit she was trying on was both elegant and practical, and it looked splendid on her. The shoulders were perfectly tailored, and the skirt flared slightly in the back. However, it seemed that close — *very* close — inspection had revealed that the skirt and jacket must have been made from different bolts of fabric, as they were almost imperceptibly dissimilar shades of blue.

Need I add that Sylvie did not buy that suit?

Although it fit her like the proverbial glove, it was fatally flawed. Sylvie's standards for how she presents herself to the world did not include wearing mismatched (however faintly) suits. Moreover, she had decided that the skirt's flirtatious flare, though indisputably à la mode, did not flatter her rear. The experience inspired me with a new determination: to examine Parisian women as closely as they obviously examine themselves. And that resolution, together with my subsequent empirical research, has led to this important announcement: *French women do too get fat.* In fact, they come in all sizes, from very slender to very stout. Here's my version of the same sentence: *French women, no matter their size, dress thin.*

I suspect that most American adolescents learn how to dress from movies and television. Their style sense imprints at a vulnerable age, just as newly hatched chicks might imprint on a broom — and with equally disastrous results. In my case, it was extremely unfortunate that *Grease* was followed by *Flashdance.* At one particularly low point, I permed my hair into a red halo that stood out four inches around my head, although I was just astute enough to grasp that skintight leather pants would not flatter my sturdy Minnesota frame. Still, for at least three or four years, sweaters constantly drooped off one of my (chilly) shoulders, and leg warmers added a good three inches to the circumference of my lower legs.

But to return to the more cheerful present, after months as a sartorial secret agent — and a few key conversations with any woman carrying a French passport who would agree to describe her closet — I can tell you definitively that young French women do not turn to Hollywood for instruction on how to dress. Instead, they discover what flatters their particular figure, and they stick with it.

My months of surveillance can be summed up in two words: time and tailoring.

Time? In my case, I've been shopping for decades, have a closet and dresser stuffed with clothes, and still don't have anything to wear — because though I take time to shop, I never give time to figuring out how to *wear* the clothes I bought. What's more, like those droopy sweaters, they often don't fit very well. In my next life, I plan to be reincarnated in the kind of body that looks good no matter what I'm wearing; if you're already one of The Blessed, feel free to skip the rest of this essay. If not, you have two choices, as I see it: (a) fearlessly investigate whether your clothes flatter your rear (and other areas) or (b) avoid all mirrors, storefronts, and female commentary. The second choice has a lot going for it, including peace of mind and a happy disposition.

Still, let's go back to choice number one. Take a look down any street in Paris and you'll almost certainly see a sign for a tailor. That's because it is *routine* to take new clothing to the tailor and have it fitted. I once had a French academic look at me as if I were out of my mind when I confessed to entering a tailor's shop only if a hem dragged behind me like a Renaissance cape. It turned out that she wouldn't dream of wearing pants without first altering the inseam, and the same goes for crucial lines in jackets, dresses, and almost anything but socks. Apparently, even lingerie stores routinely alter bras so they fit properly. Having never got over the conviction that my breasts are too small to be appreciated by women (I know this sounds peculiar, but were I a lesbian, I would definitely be chasing after women with large tatas), I've never done the bra-measuring thing. We all draw the line somewhere.

The tailor around the corner from rue du Conservatoire spends his days in a tiny room crammed with piles of fabric and un-mended garments. Over the year, I have taken almost all my clothing to him and he has altered each piece. He made a dress hit precisely where it should on my hips, altered shoulders so that they fit *my* shoulders alone, and tailored my pants' inseams to fit properly. In short, he turned ready-to-wear — prêt-à-porter — clothing into a version of couture, the luxury clothing that is made to a client's specific measurements.

And he didn't charge much, either.

It wasn't until I had spent a few months scrutinizing women — in the streets, on the Métro — that it dawned on me I had never really taken time to analyze which of my garments looked good together. I happen to own lots of shoes; I've always considered that one of the best benefits of being married to a man from Italy. Once, to take a regrettable example, I bought acid green pumps with three-inch heels in Rome, because they were chic and on sale. Back in the United States, I threw them in my closet and donned black oxfords day after day. It took some time, but I recently figured out that those green pumps work with only one dress, which happened to be rather short, verging on mini. Those three-inch green pumps? Off to Goodwill, victims of the fact that I occasionally shop as if I might still go dancing. In a club.

That leads to another important — and potentially painful — piece of advice. Once you have come up with an outfit that looks terrific, you have to be ruthless with yourself about your actual age, as opposed to how old you feel. A few months ago, Luca surveyed my décolletage and apparently found it too low, because he asked me if I was "having a young moment." Do not let this happen to you. It took me weeks to recover.

So what if you were once a pageant queen or a *Flashdance* junkie? Face it: those days are gone. An eleven-year-old girl can be remarkably handy in keeping this in perspective; Anna, for example, offers her unvarnished opinions quite freely. "I don't think that looks good on your butt," she says, stressing *think* in case I want to counter that my bottom has never looked better. "You look like an old librarian." (Don't have a live-in eleven-year-old girl, and can't beg, borrow, or steal one? I'll rent mine out at bottom rate.)

Put all the clothes that go *with* something else on the left of your closet, and those that don't on the right. Take every single piece of clothing on the right to a charity shop, and every leftover piece to a tailor. You might not have many clothes, but that's okay. Outfits are like casseroles — you only need to know how to make a couple.

As a reward, go shopping, online or in person, but only to buy any of these three indispensable items that you don't already own: a pair of black boots, a rosy scarf, or a belt. Wear the boots in all seasons except summer, the scarf close to your face, and the belt when you're feeling brave.

I just reread this essay and came to the dismal realization that you'll run into me on the street and accuse me of rabid untruthfulness because I'm not wearing a belt and my boots are red. Or because I am wearing my favorite sweatshirt, which was rejected by Luca because it is emblazoned (rather obscurely) with the word SUPERDRY.

What's more, you probably think that Sylvie is a model of elegance, sweeping through the bank in spike heels, her hair in an elegant chignon. Not so! Sylvie is the mother of three smallish children with a tiring job that involves long hours. She is not rail-thin, nor does she wear a scarf jauntily tied around her neck, no matter the season. At some point I actually asked her why she wasn't a fashion plate. She laughed and shrugged. "This is *me*," she said. "I am comfortable."

Witness my new (borrowed) philosophy: Sylvie dresses very much like my American friends in the legal and financial professions.

But there is a Parisian twist: she knows that her suit fits perfectly and flatters her figure in every possible fashion. Her style has nothing to do with high heels, and everything to do with confidence.

The other day I came across this quote from Miuccia Prada (yes, that Prada): "Being elegant isn't easy. You have to study it, like cuisine and art." To be honest, I'm not going for my dissertation in the field. I (and perhaps you as well) will never be a *chef de couture.* We don't need to be — any more than Sylvie does. All we have to do is give the process enough time and tailoring so that we are true to our own figures.

And then we can admire (if from afar) those Parisiennes who achieve a doctorate in the subject.

Saint Catherine is the French patron saint of unmarried women. Her feast day, November 25, used to be celebrated by working-class girls who would take a day off and don homemade fancy hats and their very best clothing. Supposedly, the parties held on that night were their last chance to meet Monsieur Charmant. Recently I jogged into a tiny park called Square Montholon and collapsed, panting, on a bench in front of a statue of five young women in Edwardian costumes celebrating Saint Catherine's Day. Rain dripped from the trees and rolled down their cheeks, and it seemed as if they'd been caught in a storm while wearing their best clothing.

The Musée de l'Armée on rue de Grenelle has a lovely formal garden off to one side, made up of paths lined with topiaries shaped into small cones. It looks like the Queen of Hearts' gardens in *Alice's Adventures in Wonderland:* old-fashioned, elaborately trimmed, slightly askew, and slightly crazy.

The new girl (and five boys) arrived at Luca's tennis camp today: tragically, she is only eleven years old. There will be no final dance, a highlight of last year. Plus, it snowed in the Italian mountains, so they haven't even been able to play much tennis. Dreams of both romance and athletic prowess have been smashed.

Anna just called, very excited, to say that she's bought Domitilla a going-away present: toy guinea pigs that move and squeak, along with their guinea-pig house and their guinea-pig car. Alessandro says that, at fifty-nine euros, the present took half the money she'd managed to save from gifts and her allowance in the last year. I've met mothers who told stories of their children's selfless, generous natures, but I've never joined the chorus, for good reason. This is my first such boastful announcement. I'm very, very proud of her.

After a year in Paris, and multiple dispiriting experiences eating criminally bad food, I've come to the conclusion that the legendary brasseries — the ones where the waiters wear long aprons and the lamps pretend to be fueled by gas — should be avoided at all costs. The final straw: a friend took me to the Bofinger brasserie, a restaurant that felt about as authentic as Epcot's version of the Eiffel Tower. (One big difference: the food at Epcot is terrific.) I thought my fish risotto tasted fishy, and after enduring three days of nausea, I'm sure of it.

I just bought six small china ramekins, three pale asparagus and three dark plum, at our local hardware store. They have delicate handles and were made for crème brûlée, but I'm going to make individual lemon tarts in them, and dust them with sugar through a fleur-de-lis stencil — which I discovered in the same place. Hardware stores offer far better souvenirs than tourist shops can dream of; every time you use your hot pink whisk, for example, it will remind you of Paris.

Last night I came down rue Richer at eight o'clock, when the light starts to go golden and the shopkeepers hang out on their doorsteps, ready to lock up. Prancing in front of me was a three-year-old in a candy-stripe dress, white shoes with butterflies, and hot pink sunglasses perched on her head. She was stopping before each shop-keeper to call *"Bonsoir!"* while her mother waited patiently with the stroller.

With the family in Italy, no one interrupts me; there are no squabbles; there isn't any laundry. My academic book grows every day, and my Lose-Parisian-Pounds diet is on track. The problem is, I just can't sleep. My body knows all this silence and empty space is wrong. The light around the curtains this morning was colorless, like the froth on a wave, as if even that signaled the absence of what matters most.

Today I succumbed to rampant curiosity about Claude's life, and actually telephoned my uncle Malcolm back in Minnesota.

(Malcolm was one of Claude's nephews.) It turns out that Claude mostly wrote literary fiction, but he tried genre fiction as well; Malcolm recalled, for example, a novella about a paranormal device that turned parts of Duluth into a tropical paradise. Claude's father was convinced that his son had remarkable literary talent and set up a trust that allowed him to enjoy an intellectual life in Italian villas. (The comparison with my mother is painful, but I'm consoling myself with the fact that if Mom had had the cash, she would certainly have underwritten my literary attempts, whether she considered them deserving or not.) Claude died on a trip to Minnesota, when he went fishing with the author Sinclair Lewis and caught a staph infection. Claude, Uncle Malcolm concluded, "was effete in the sense of outdoor stuff like fishing." I've always hated fishing. I may parallel Claude in many ways, but this last is one I intend to avoid.

This evening I stopped at Number 37 rue des Martyrs, the uninspiringly named Bar le Select. I sat down outside and drank a glass of excellent wine. In the States, I would feel odd drinking alone at a bar, but here it feels absolutely natural. I happily watched poodles and Parisians parade past.

I am alone in the most enchanting city in the world, and at this moment, it's as if the locals strut by just for my pleasure.

Tennis camp finished yesterday, and the kids are in Florence with Marina for a few days before returning to Paris. "I lost the tournament, Mama," Anna reported last night. Then she perked up: "But I hit my teacher with a ball right in the forehead!"

Today I reached a landmark: I am back to my weight before I encountered the vast and luscious temptations of Paris. And that's a good thing, because I happened past the atelier of Joséphine Vannier, the chocolate artisan who made my wonderful Cinderella shoe. She also creates boxes made entirely from dark chocolate and decorated in edible paint. They are about the size of small jewelry boxes; I bought one in amethyst, with meticulously painted gold curlicues on top.

Alessandro is now back in Florence after two weeks in the mountains with Milo, who was given no prosciutto treats for the duration, a cruel hardship indeed. Marina counted up and weighed the 80 diet food pellets that Alessandro had been giving him each day and announced that Milo had been starved, because the vet had prescribed 120. Everyone calmed down after Milo was hoisted on the scale and discovered to have lost . . . nothing. *Niente.* A sumo wrestler would be proud to have such a metabolism.

I'm going to a big writers' conference in Florida in a few weeks, and I'm anticipating being cold, because I know the hotel will be air-conditioned to arctic levels. To be prepared, I've bought a charcoal gray coat made of crinkly material that you can roll up and shove in a handbag without ruining it. It's Japanese, frightfully sophisticated — and 100 percent polyester. When I was growing up, *polyester* was practically a four-letter word.

Since I'm alone, I'm not bothering to cook, and luckily the frozen food store, Picard, sells heavenly heat-and-eat meals. But today I bought a fresh entrée in Monoprix because the esteemed chef Joël Robuchon "made" it. Out of the box, it turned out to be a little casserole in an adorable china baking ramekin.

We are a No-Electronic-Games-System household. Anna called up from Italy, very

302

excited. "Mama, I had a vision!" I inquired about this miraculous event. "I was staring into space, and suddenly I just saw myself playing the new Harry Potter game. The portable one." Her vision will never become reality, but I do love how she claimed paranormal backup.

I went to the Musée Jacquemart-André by myself today. On my earlier visits, I was accompanied by friends and the audiotape; this time, though, I was responsible for no one's happiness but my own, and wandered in silence through all the rooms. I am very fond of a marble statue of a little girl rather improbably caressing a dove. Although she's stark naked, her hair is elaborately braided and fixed with a bow. I love her plump tummy and stubby toes.

Alessandro and the children are back from Italy. We had sushi last night instead of frozen food, and I slept until 6:30 instead of 5:00. Anna has figured out what she wants to be when she grows up — a cake decorator. "I absolutely *looove* fondant," she told me. Then she asked whether you have to go to college to decorate cakes. Absolutely. Haven't you heard of that class? Fondant 101.

■ ■ ■ ■

The idiotic workmen on the floor above us just loaded a heavy bag of cement into our tiny elevator, causing all the cables to snap. It plunged five floors to the ground and has to be completely rebuilt — a repair that is scheduled to take place in August. *After we leave.* We're looking at three whole weeks of four flights of stairs going down, and four flights going up. Hauling groceries upstairs without an elevator is one thing; the idea of *moving out* without an elevator makes me want to run up a flight and turn into a profanity-spewing American she-devil — the kind seen in foreign films and sometimes homegrown films, too. *The Devil Wears French Underwear.*

It's intolerably hot in Paris. My study is a little room sandwiched between our bedroom and the living room. It has one set of big windows, looking directly into the sun. So I drew the curtains. Now the room is hot and dark, like a sauna version of the Bat Cave. I just stripped to my bra and undies, and I'm still too hot to write.

Home from Italian tennis camp, Luca is

putting up a strenuous battle against going to the French equivalent. This is all to no avail, as it's already been paid for, but he won't stop arguing about it. I know he's scared stiff, but I look at his cheekbones and remind myself that French women — no matter how young — are connoisseurs of male beauty. He'll be fine.

Friends Kim, Paul, and Summer are visiting from New York. Summer is a bewitching eight-year-old with the peaked chin and wild laughter of a wood elf — basically, an Anna doppelgänger. Within hours, they were holding hands, wreathing their arms around each other while walking. At bedtime, Anna informed me that Summer is different from other girls. "How so?" I asked. "She doesn't do what I say." I suggested that Summer may be even more fun to play with because she has her own ideas. Anna is still thinking this over.

There are places in the world that do not live up to their billing; Giverny, the site of Monet's blurry, lovely paintings, is not one of them. We are just back in Paris after being enchanted by water lilies with deep pink hearts, poppies with translucent pink petals, cascades of coral roses. This may be heresy,

305

but I think that Monet's gardens are more beautiful in reality than they are in paint.

Today Anna went to camp, so Kim and I dropped Summer off in a park with her dad while we went shopping. Returning later to collect them, we were met with a forked stick jutting from a mound of earth, pale green leaves flapping in the wind like tiny sails. "A funeral mound," Summer announced. We looked respectfully at the grave, which turned out to house a deceased Tic Tac. RIP.

Last night our visiting friends took us to a two-star Michelin restaurant, Carré des Feuillants. We began with flutes of rose-colored champagne and white asparagus. I had flaky turbot dressed with a thin line of caviar. The black-on-white effect made me think of a chic wedding cake, but it tasted delicately of the sea, of butter and cream: the very cooking that made Julia Child fall in love with France.

Alessandro hauled Luca, protesting every inch of the way, to Gare de Lyon to catch a train to French tennis camp. In the campers' designated waiting area, Alessandro overheard another father say something in

Italian to his son, but Luca wouldn't allow him to make contact. "I think he's embarrassed by me," Alessandro told me morosely. You *think?*

We just visited a jewelry workshop, Commelin, which began making charms, by hand, in 1880. Even though it's not a retail store, they welcome visitors. We watched an artisan creating exquisite enameled squares that will someday become a chessboard. I succumbed, and started charm bracelets for Anna and my two nieces with teeny gold Eiffel Towers.

Paris is so hot that the white plaster walls of the building opposite my study window shimmer, slightly out of focus, as if they belonged on an Aegean island overlooking the sea. We have no air-conditioning, and of course the elevator is still broken. Yesterday the construction workers who broke the elevator smashed one of the stained-glass windows in the stairwell. For the first time, I can think about leaving Paris without feeling a pang of sadness.

For years, Anna's biggest ambition has been to have five children and live in the suburbs with a new minivan. Whenever she mentions this, she generally throws in a petition for a younger sibling. We have visitors right now who include three children — ages two, six, and eight. Anna just told me that she's not having any children, ever.

One of our visitors, Damiano, is a six-year-old with Down syndrome who has captured Alessandro's heart. Walking down the street, Damiano holds Alessandro's hand tightly. Whenever there are stairs to be navigated, he unfolds his arms upward with a beaming smile, as if he were a sunflower and Alessandro the sun. And my husband melts and scoops him up, every time.

Luca just texted from his camp in the French Alps — the Tour de France whizzed through, and he saw Lance Armstrong! At least, he thinks he saw Lance; it was all a blur. It sounds as if the bicycles were zooming down the mountain buzzing like evicted hornets.

The sun was shining as I went out for a run this morning. I had scarcely entered the door back at home when the sky went dark and rain started to pummel the street. Across from my study it sluiced down the gray roofs, pouring onto hapless pedestrians below, and bounced white off the street.

Alessandro and I just babysat Damiano and his siblings while their parents did some sightseeing. Damiano caught us hugging and decided he wanted to see more. With an impish grin, he kept finding Alessandro and tugging his hand to bring him wherever I was, so Alessandro could give me a hug and a kiss. And then Damiano would climb in my lap to do the same. It was a very blessed afternoon.

Last night, we sat at a café and watched as a gentleman in his eighties asked a young woman if she was the pharmacist across the street. Then he pulled out a condom and asked how much they cost in her pharmacy. Seeing everyone around him grinning, he gave us a smirk (and a figurative twirl of his mustache) and said, "These things are getting more expensive every day! I'm going to her pharmacy, if they're as cheap as she says."

Luca called from French tennis camp, which is apparently far, far better than Italian camp. For one thing, there are girls. *French* girls. Didn't this salient fact occur to him when he was making our life miserable insisting that he would not go and we couldn't make him?

Today is rainy, cool, and windy. The sky is silvery gray, like the watered silk skirts of a Victorian lady, long widowed, and still regretful.

I am going to miss French supermarkets. Things I adore: fresh gazpacho and cucumber soups (found next to the orange juice), chicken bouillon in muslin sachets, ditto bouquets garnis, and individual servings of pesto, perfect for quick pasta.

Yesterday I had a little party for my French readers. We had pink champagne garnished with red currants, and pink cookies, and talked about books and children and Paris. And Anna politely chatted with my guests! She did not read, although her Harry Potter book was hidden at her back throughout.

ROSE

A few years ago a friend invited me to her house to meet another friend of hers, an academic named Rose, who was being treated for recurrent ovarian cancer, had read my romances, and wanted to meet me. I'm fairly familiar with this phenomenon: people who pride themselves on negotiating (for example) the thousand-plus pages of David Foster Wallace's *Infinite Jest* turn to romance fiction when they can no longer bear the smell of bleach, the tick of the IV, and the bad news.

So I girded my loins for a less than cheerful encounter with an emaciated and wan cancer patient. But instead, Rose sat at the head of the table, round and rosy, bellowing with laughter and wearing a huge platinum Marilyn Monroe wig. I learned later that her own hair was black and she wore it cropped short and standing straight up, bleached on the ends so she looked like a blown dandelion. But she liked to wear the Marilyn wig now and then because, as she explained, it's impossible to pity a woman wearing a stylized wave of 1950s curls. At least not because of her terminal status.

I fell in love with her wig and her laugh — outward signs of remarkable courage. We became BFFs, with all the irony that term implies. Every once in a while Rose's doctors would make noises about how perhaps the day had come when the cancer had finally beat out the chemo. But then they would try a different drug, and through it all she kept teaching, and translating poetry, and traveling to Latin America to discover new poets. Once she called me from the top of a Peruvian mountain. She sounded as if she were next door. "It's so beautiful here," she said. "You must come before you die."

Rose wasn't afraid to say that. She had the gift of knowing, very concretely, that her time was limited, though she certainly didn't welcome the end. She loved the Dominican Republic, and one year we flew to a resort, just the two of us. The next year we went to the island again, but to a different resort, one she had found online that titled itself Paradise.

Paradise's claims to be heaven on earth were somewhat exaggerated (the presence of a number of classy prostitutes added an obvious complication), but we had a wonderful time. We swam with dolphins, who were supremely uninterested in us but wildly captivating, like the most beautiful people at a New York cocktail party. We had massages in a small garden walled with flowering trees, and kicked around on the beach at twilight. We drank margaritas, and Rose recited poetry to me in Spanish, a language I do not speak. She was always recommending Latin American novelists and poets, and I always promised to read them, and I never did.

Even then, after years of fighting cancer, she was beautiful: lush, charismatic, full of charm. "I think that waiter has a crush on me," she told me. And she was right, about him and about our taxi driver, too. Dominicans looked straight past me — tall, thin, pale, boring — but their faces lit up when they met Rose. She burst with life and Spanish and shining skin. They didn't have the slightest idea she was dying.

But we both knew that trip to Paradise would be our last together. Rose came to see us in New Jersey just before we departed for France, in June. Loving soul that she was, she had never breathed a word about the unfairness of my optimistic prognosis in comparison to hers, the fact that doctors whisked away my cancer and set me free to live in Paris while they could not conquer hers. We did talk about the fearsome oddness of the two of us — and my mother — being diagnosed with cancer. It felt like a crapshoot, but the black number seemed to be turning up with terrifying regularity.

By this point, Rose had decided to refuse further treatment, and instead she was touring hospices, with as much focused interest as she had researched resorts in the Dominican Republic. I knew it was her decision to make, but I felt selfish, too. I managed to stop myself from pleading with her to reconsider that decision, but I did beg her to visit us.

She shook her head. "I'll call you," she told me, "when you need to come." Her phone call asking me to fly back came sooner than I had imagined, just a few months into the fall.

My mother had been supremely courageous at the end, a stance made easier because she was completely looped on painkillers. She drifted away as drunk as a lord: she told me that there were horses galloping on her covers and tangling with her toes. One night I handed her the phone so that she could speak to my sister, far away in New Jersey. "Why are you parked in a car at the end of my driveway?" she demanded. Her last days were full of imagination; she said that a beloved brother, dead some eight years, was waiting for her in the hallway.

In that situation, one weeps for oneself. "I'm having a good death," she announced, a few days before she stopped talking.

But Rose . . . Rose did not have a good death. As it happened, the first day I arrived at the hospice she took that miracle drug, whatever it is, and informed me with a giggle that there were tiny blue butterflies dancing all around my head. But for her the side effects turned out to be even worse than the pain — which meant no more butterflies, no galloping horses . . . just the clear awareness that death was agonizing days or hours away. The last thing my mother had said to me was that I had a beautiful smile. I'm not sure whether she knew exactly who I was at that moment, but I was so happy to have given her that smile. The last thing Rose said to me was goodbye.

I told her as ferociously as I could that I expected her to wait for me on the other side of whatever bridge she was about to cross. "Do you hear me, Rose?" I demanded. There were tears sliding down her face. She loved Anna and Luca almost as much as Alessandro and I do, so I made her promise that she would meet my children, too, if by some awful twist they went before me. And then there was nothing else to say, so I cried my way down the corridor of the hospice, into my rental car, and back to the airport.

Rose died a few days later, having said goodbye to everyone, tidied up her affairs, and found a home for her cat.

A short time later, back in Paris, a book-size parcel arrived for me. It was from Rose, a last dash of the loving attention she gave so freely. It took me a while to force myself to open that package: I couldn't bear that it was the last letter, the last present. I thought she had sent me one of those Latin American novels I always promised to read. But instead it was W. G. Sebald's *Austerlitz,* a novel about grief, memory, the longing to remember, and the longing to forget.

I have spent this year in a kind of Paradise, though one without dolphins or beaches or mountaintops. I often thought of Rose — her Marilyn curls, her big laugh, her fearless *before you die* — while I walked the streets of Paris, and I missed her.

The impetus to move to Paris, to sell the house and the cars and simply fly away, sprang from my mother's death and my own brush with cancer. But I wonder if I would have acted on the idea without lessons learned from Rose.

So this book is my phone call — not from the top of a mountain, or even the top of the Eiffel Tower: the "here" is negotiable.

It's so beautiful here. You must come before you die.

This morning Anna said, casually, "I'll make myself breakfast." Afterward she reported washing her plate and glass. When I asked if she wanted me to run a bath, she said, "No, I'll do it." It was like seeing a movie version of Eloise, in which she suddenly leapt ahead ten years — delightful and frightening at the same time. Though, of course, Eloise would be terrifying at any age.

Yesterday we went to the huge flea market, Clignancourt, looking for a special object to remind us of Paris. We were wandering around looking at antiques when we found a do-it-yourself chandelier store. You choose a base, and then add colored fruits in Bohemian crystal. Their examples seemed to suggest that restraint, color-wise, was a good idea: a chandelier in red and gold, say, or blue and violet. We started with a brass base, and then added violet and gold pears, glowing red bunches of grapes, amber apples, and strings of crystals. It's crazily wonderful.

Luca has a best friend at camp, a boy who sounds like a caricature of an emotional Frenchman. "He has a crush on this girl," Luca reported. "And I kind of do, too. I think she may be looking at me. But I told him that I would back off." Behind-the-scenes détente, teenage division.

Anna is on Chapter Eight of the novel she's been working on, a riveting tale of naughty children and a runaway pig. Recently she added a new character, a frilly French orphan named Lucille, and today she proposed a chapter that would flash back to Lucille's mother reading to her. "Too sad," I objected. "Mama," Anna said impatiently, "this is a novel! There has to be some crying."

Our last night in Paris . . . Florent suggested dinner at one of his favorite restaurants as a way to celebrate our year. Apparently he and Pauline went there for a proper date, post–lemon tart. Le Bistrot du Peintre turned out to be an old-fashioned French bistro on avenue Ledru-Rollin — small and Art Nouveauish — that hasn't succumbed to the tourist trade and was crowded with Parisians. I had a gazpacho, followed by delicate haddock and new potatoes in a mustard vinaigrette that I thought about all the way home. It was a splendid way to say goodbye to a fabulous year.

Driving back to Florence, we stopped for a night in Beaune, a beautiful walled city in Burgundy. For supper Luca had escargots, which smelled so wonderful that Anna begged and pleaded for one. I was looking at the menu and said, "Anna, look, they have ice cream!" She wailed, "I don't want ice cream; I want snails!" We ordered more escargots, and champagne (without orange juice) to celebrate: a year in Paris has done wonders for our children.

Overnight, we have gone from the sublime (Beaune, France) to the ridiculous (Pavia, Italy). Rather than a splendid four-star hotel, we could find rooms only in a dingy hotel on a strip, with ripped holes in the towels (the first time I've seen that!). And rather than snails, we ate at Grillandia, where they were having Spanish night, with buxom, faux-Spanish dancers and a rice mix from a box. Even Anna allowed that she missed Paris.

Before we leave Pavia, we are dragging our less-than-enthusiastic children to see the tomb of Saint Augustine, after which we will drive the three hours to Florence, back to Marina and Milo. Marina said defensively on the phone last night that we shouldn't expect to see a thinner Milo, because it's too hot in Florence to expect a dog to diet. Some things never change.

THE END

When I'm writing a novel, typing "The End" is the best moment of all, because by then I'm desperate to be finished — generally late for my deadline, exhausted, unkempt, and irritable. Yet I'm reluctant to type the final page of *Paris in Love*. Putting these last words on paper brings a close to an experience that I hate to see slip into the past, even though as I write this essay, we've been living in New York City for almost a year. But of course, even while we lived on rue du Conservatoire, time was slipping through our hands. Alessandro and I had jobs to which we had to return, but we had nowhere to live. We had sold our house and cars, planning to buy an apartment . . . sometime.

After Christmas, we both realized with a jolt that the time had come. Two very nice realtors named Curtis and William lined up a series of apartment visits for us. Somewhat to their consternation, we decided to give the search exactly three days. We flew in on a Friday in February, and by five o'clock that afternoon we were inspecting apartments in the peculiar state of anxiety that goes along with buying something costing approximately the same as a small Polynesian island. Maybe even one that comes with a village or two. We were dazed by jet lag, but not enough to overlook the fact that the first apartment we saw was the only one in our size and price range located in our preferred neighborhood. And it had a long built-in bookshelf. Nevertheless, in the interests of due diligence, we spent the rest of the weekend struggling up and down Broadway in a snowstorm, tramping our way into strangers' living rooms. But nothing appealed after that first one; I compared every bookshelf to the first, and found them lacking. On Monday morning, we went to see our realtors and put in a bid. The experience was surreal; our mortgage was going to be so huge it felt like Monopoly money. And the next morning we discovered that our offer was accepted.

But we still faced the dreaded co-op approval process. In New York, most people don't really buy their apartments; they merely buy shares in a co-op. And before the members of a co-op board deem you worthy to live within their hallowed walls, they have the right to see all your financial records (and when I say all, I mean going back to your first job at DeToy's Supper Club), not to mention the fact you have to pass a personal interview with the board, as do your children and, if you've got one, your dog. We flew back in May for the co-op interview, knowing that the outcome was by no means a foregone conclusion: in fact, William and Curtis were a bit depressed when we arrived, since a co-op board had inexplicably turned down another of their clients that very morning. They left us on the doorstep with a few final, anxious bits of advice about not venturing any unasked-for personal details because almost anything might trigger someone's dislike. It seemed obvious that prejudice and personal bias could hold sway — and with impunity. We hoped there was no one in the bunch who hated romance writers. Or literature professors. Yale alumni! Italians! The possibilities were endless.

(I must add here that only one thing had scared me more than the co-op board, and that was the bedbug epidemic in New York. Even over in Paris, we'd heard that the entire city was crawling with them. Happily,

I no longer had worries about this particular apartment, because at the same time we'd allowed the co-op board to ransack our financial history, demand numerous personal recommendations, and even interview our children by Skype, we asked for one, and only one, thing in return: the right for our lawyer to scour the minutes of co-op board meetings, going back decades, in search of that panic-inducing word: *bedbugs.* It was nowhere to be found.)

At the inquisition, once we'd cleared up a few questions (such as whether I had to return a publisher's advance if one of my books failed — the answer is no), I began to feel cautiously optimistic. Everybody was smiling. They were talking about holiday parties. Then the chair of the co-op board leaned forward and said, "There is *nothing* personal about this question, but I'm afraid that I do have to ask whether you have been in contact with bedbugs." Alessandro broke out laughing and explained my deep-rooted phobia, the only factor that would have made us turn down an apartment as lovely as this one. At which point an older gentleman piped up, "Oh, you shouldn't be so scared; I had them last year." As it happened, the interview was taking place in his very apartment. Every head at the table

whipped around to stare at him. He nodde
to a door at his shoulder. "They came in a
suitcase that had been incorrectly routed
through Bolivia," he said cheerfully. "We
figured it out when a guest staying in our
guest room got bitten, so we had them taken
care of."

Alessandro gave me a sharp kick — the
marital equivalent of *don't scream* — but I
was too shocked to respond anyway. I was
thinking that this apartment was directly
below the one we'd just bought. "How long
ago did you say this happened?" the board
chair asked, in what I considered an admira-
bly controlled manner. I emerged from a
sickening panic attack only when I realized
that the conversation had moved on, and
now concerned a person living in the building who apparently did not always take his
medication. The board was giving us a
heads-up about his occasionally erratic
behavior. "He can be rather abrupt with
children," one member said, "and they may
think he's attacking them, but he's really
not aggressive." "He's our lamb, our com-
munity project," someone else offered.
"He's never attacked *my* children," said a
third. "Then you're lucky," the first board
member shot back.

We reeled out into the snow and walked

recisely one block before I stopped to call our realtors and babble into the phone about bedbugs and unmedicated crazy people. Eventually, Alessandro managed to drag me away from the phone (by then I had Curtis listing pest control agencies that would *guarantee* total annihilation) and into a restaurant. Once I had a glass of wine in hand, my husband pointed out that a person doesn't move to New York City if she really wants to be living in a placid, vermin-free suburb. We were moving to the city precisely so that we would never have to conduct another conversation about weed trimmers or oil changes. We would have other, more thrilling, subjects of discussion: to wit, bedbugs and schizophrenics.

It took a while, but I came to see his point.

New York would be an adventure, whereas New Jersey (for us) had been an existence. As it happened, our apartment proved to be, indeed, free from bedbugs, and we have come to know many, if not all, of the people in our building . . . without ever identifying the person who may or may not be taking his medication.

In the past year, I have discovered the shop of a chocolate artisan half a block from the apartment. I have been asked (most politely) if there are any devils standing beside me on the subway platform. I have survived not bedbugs but *three* separate infestations of lice, mercifully limited to the younger members of the family. I have used my Parisian cocottes to make chocolate cakes, and worn my black boots to department meetings. Anna embraced the city happily, and Luca (who now says he is going to college in France) announces on a regular basis that he hates it. Though the children have reversed places, the opposition feels cozily familiar.

Paris in Love is about a tremendously joyful year, one that I sometimes remember now through a rosy haze of chocolate and lingerie. But the joy didn't come from chocolate alone. Surrounded by people speaking a different language, our family started talking to each other. We drew into a very small tribe (population: four), who ate together, and squabbled together, and mostly played together. We learned to waste our moments — together.

And then we brought that lesson home with us.

ACKNOWLEDGMENTS

Many people played a role in bringing *Paris in Love* to print. Carrie Feron was the first to tell me that our adventures in Paris should be turned into a book. The terrific food blog One for the Table published an early version of the Christmas essay. My fierce and fabulous agent, Kim Witherspoon, championed the project, and my brilliant editor, Susan Kamil, instantly understood it, gave it a home, and lent her perfect pitch to moments of both humor and sadness. Anne Connell painstakingly read every word and improved the text immeasurably. I was lucky that many wonderful people at Random House devoted so much time to designing and launching this memoir. I owe all of you a debt of deep gratitude. And finally, I would like to thank the friends and readers who begged me to tell them more stories of Paris: your enthusiasm taught me a new way to write.

MY VERY IDIOSYNCRATIC GUIDE TO A FEW PLACES IN PARIS

A SHORT LIST OF SMALL MUSEUMS WORTH SEEING

Only you know whether you have the stamina for the Louvre and d'Orsay museums. I myself do not. I enjoy museums that take an hour or so to go through. Rather than try to rush past 300,000 paintings in the Louvre, or, worse, shoving aside your fellow tourists to see the *Mona Lisa,* you can wander through these museums in relative comfort.

Musée Claude Monet à Giverny. Monet's foundation at Giverny is easy to reach by train from Paris. Take the Paris-to-Vernon train, and then the shuttle bus from Vernon to Giverny (just follow the crowd). The train leaves every two hours or so, and the shuttle meets it. They have a gift store that displays an earnest belief that water lilies enhance everything from aprons to encils. *www.fondation-monet.fr/fr*

Les Arts Decoratifs. This is a small museum connected to the Louvre devoted to decorative arts — furniture, china, accessories. There are many reasons to go here: the collection of 1960s furniture, the collection of 1800s furniture, fascinating revolving exhibits . . . and the appealing fact that there is generally no line. *www.lesarts decoratifs.fr*

Musée Jacquemart-André. My favorite museum in all of Paris. I mention some of the collection in this book. Be sure to get the audiotape; I actually listened to all the "extra" sections, and they were worth it. Afterward, have lunch or tea in the **Salon de Thé,** which is located in the house's original dining room (there's an incredible Tiepolo ceiling). 158 boulevard Haussmann. *www.musee-jacquemart-andre.com*

Musée de la Vie Romantique. To be honest, this museum doesn't have anything utterly fabulous in it — no Renoirs or Fragonards. But it's a preserved home from the 1800s and is fascinating in its own right; George Sand's drawing room, for example, is beautiful. It's small, and there's a terrific tea shop in the garden where the kids can dash about. 16 rue Chaptal. *www.vie-romantique.paris.fr*

Musée Nissim de Camondo. One of my favorite museums; don't miss it. Not only are Count Moïse de Camondo's possessions fascinating, but his story is heartbreaking. And the French have not shrunk from depicting the truth of what happened to his family during World War II. Be sure to get the audio guide. 63 rue de Monceau. *www.lesartsdecoratifs.fr/francais/nissim-de-camondo*

Plus, when you walk through **Parc Monceau** from the Métro, keep an eye out for brides. The park in front of Musée Nissim de Camondo is one of the favorite places for bridal pictures.

After the museum, recover your spirits by walking back through the park and then stopping at **La Table Monceau.** It's not fancy, but the food is great, and the clientele are all French, which is always interesting (1 rue de Phalsbourg). If you'd rather have a cup of tea and an excellent pastry, walk from Parc Monceau down boulevard de Courcelles to **La Petite Rose,** a charming little patisserie. I met a friend here for tea. We sat for hours discussing everything from babies to dementia (one leads naturally to the other). The pastries are wonderful. 11 boulevard de Courcelles.

Musée Carnavalet. This is the museum of Paris. It can be summed up as a lot of separate rooms full of furniture that were bought outright and stuck into a jumbled-up museum. As that description implies, Carnavalet doesn't really belong on a list of small museums; after a while, you might find yourself staggering with exhaustion. So don't get encyclopedic; just take a look at the rooms devoted to the reigns of Kings Louis XV and XVI. 23 rue de Sévigné. *www.carnavalet.paris.fr*

In the Marais. I am putting together a list of a few places in the Marais because so often people don't have a week — let alone a year — to enjoy Paris. If you have only twenty-four hours, the Marais is a good place to go; a plus is that the stores are open on Sundays.

IN THE MARAIS
Brunch at **Des Gars dans la Cuisine.** You must have a reservation. Try to sit in the window and watch everyone prancing by. 72 rue Vieille-du-Temple. *www.desgarsdans*

Ironically enough, my favorite store in the Marais, **Noriem,** is Japanese. They make incredible crinkled-fabric coats that you can sling over anything and always look elegant — plus they're machine-washable and never crease (because they're already creased). Expensive, but worth every penny. 27 rue Vieille-du-Temple in the Marais; they have another address as well, 4 rue du Pas-de-la-Mule. *www.noriem.fr*

Joséphine Vannier. A fabulous creator of *"chocolat artisanal"* — chocolate shaped like shoes or made into fabulous keepsake boxes (for eating). 4 rue du Pas-de-la-Mule. *www.chocolatsvannier.com*

Breizh Café Crêperie. You can't leave Paris without eating a crepe (or many); the best place we went to for crepes was Breizh Café. True, the waiters were dressed in striped "Breton" shirts that gave it an Epcot feel, but the crepes are terrific. 109 rue Vieille-du-Temple. *www.breizhcafe.com*

Amorino. Alessandro, like all Italians, is an ice-cream snob. He used to howl when we lived in New Jersey because my favorite flavor is Baskin-Robbins Rocky Road (so

hoot me: I love it). After much experimen-
tation, he decided that Amorino had the
best gelato in Paris. They also make bonbons. You choose the colors: say, an assortment of four different shapes of purple
candies packed in a violet-colored box with
a cherub on top. The lines are formidable,
but it's worth it. 31 rue Vieille-du-Temple.
www.amorino.com

SHOPPING

Dominique Denaive. I discovered this
little jewelry store by wandering in from the
street. It's unique and rather fabulous —
she makes all her pieces from resin, shaping
bracelets and necklaces in bright colors. I
have a bright blue necklace with silver accents. This is a great place to buy a present;
they package your purchase in a little velvet
drawstring bag. 7 rue du 29 Juillet (very
close to the Louvre). *www.denaive.com*

**Maroquinerie Saint-Honoré/B. Biberon
& Fils.** This store is on rue Saint-Honoré,
which means that it nestles right among
some staggeringly expensive boutiques. At
any rate, this one is quite different: loads of
bags in every shape and color, very reasonably priced. I bought a hot pink bag that
converts to a backpack; now I use it for

walking through Central Park. 334 ru
Saint-Honoré.

Hôtel Drouot. This is one of France's great
auction houses — and much more fun than
Christie's, because its items are often af-
fordable (my favorites: boxes that they open
on the spot, with bidders pawing at the
books and screaming their bids). To actually
buy something you need two days, because
you have to go to the showing one day and
bid on the next. I think it's much more fun
than the flea markets. 9 rue Drouot. *www
.drouot.com*

Afterward, have lunch at **J'Go Drouot.**
The restaurant is full of seasoned auction
dealers, so it's fun to overhear conversations
(if you understand French); the cassoulet is
excellent. 4 rue Drouot. *www.lejgo.com*

FOOD

Käramell. A lovely bonbon shop, featuring
Scandinavian candy. 15 rue des Martyrs.
www.karamell.fr

Café de la Paix. This looks like one of
those ubiquitous boxed-in-with-glass places,
but it's really splendid inside, and the hot
chocolate is amazing. Avoid the glass box
and head into the hotel itself. You can order

om the menu at Le Bar du Grand Hotel while sprawled in deep, soft chairs. Sit for a while resting your feet and admiring the domed glass ceiling. Mind you, it costs almost twenty euros for a couple of Oranginas. 5 place de l'Opéra. *www.cafedelapaix.fr*

Rose Bakery. This is a lovely little bakery that serves excellent quiche — a good place to meet someone for lunch or coffee. They have two locations, at 46 rue des Martyrs in the 9th and 30 rue Debelleyme in the 3rd.

Mariage Frères: Maison de Thé à Paris. There are various locations around Paris, one in the Marais (30–32–35 rue du Bourg-Tibourg) and another at 17 place de la Madeleine. They were founded in 1854, and still measure out your tea on a brass scale. Go pick out a crazy-named tea — Golden Monkey King or Moon Palace — and take it home to enjoy. This was the shop at which we bought my father Thé des Poètes Solitaires. *www.mariagefreres.com*

Le Bistrot du Peintre. This is a little bistro recommended by Florent, who takes his dates here. I had duck the first time, and it was so good I had precisely the same thing the second. 116 avenue Ledru-Rollin. www.bistrotdupeintre.com

Ladurée. If you're going to eat at Ladurée on the Champs-Élysées, call and make sure that your reservation is for upstairs — downstairs, particularly the glassed-in part, is shabby and disappointing. But upstairs you can pretend you're French royalty. Strangely enough (given that they are famous for their madeleines), the food is better than the desserts — except those madeleines, which are fabulous. 16 rue Royale. *www.laduree.fr*

À la Mère de Famille. A wonderful bonbon store. 35 rue du Faubourg-Montmartre. *www.lameredefamille.com*

Autour du Saumon. These little salmon shops/restaurants are all over the city. We went to 56 rue des Martyrs, in the 9th. They have ten kinds of salmon — who knew? If you happen to have a kitchen in Paris, buy their table scraps and make pasta sauce. *www.autourdusaumon.eu*

Les Petites Chocolatières. This little store sells chocolate, but they also sell fantastic salted caramels. They have two locations,

37 rue des Martyrs, and 20 rue Cler. *www*
.lespetiteschocolatieres.com

La Fourmi Ailée. A bistro near Notre-
Dame with a charming blue front. It used
to be a feminist library, and it's still lined
with books. We had trouble finding restaurants around Notre-Dame that could admit
a wheelchair (many of them are actually
below street level, so you go down a few
steps). If you're in need of disabled access,
this one is great. I had a salad, and truly
spectacular sorbet. 8 rue du Fouarre, Saint-
Michel.

Saveurs & Coïncidences. A brilliant new
restaurant started by a young chef who apparently semifinaled in a nationwide culinary competition (I assume at a much
higher level than *Hell's Kitchen*). 6 rue de
Trévise. *www.saveursetcoincidences.com*

And finally, just in case you venture out of
Paris in the direction of the castles, don't
miss **La Chocolatière Royale** in Orléans.
It was the preferred chocolate maker to the
monarchy before the revolution. You can
buy a perfect rose in chocolate, or chocolate
coins stamped with Joan of Arc's picture.
51 rue Royale, Orléans. *www.lachocolatiere*
45.com

CLOTHING

For lingerie, I suggest you go to **Galeries Lafayette** and try on a load of different bras before you find the perfect label for your shape. For me, it turned out to be **Aubade,** which sells its fantastic (and fantastically expensive) bras on 33 rue des Francs-Bourgeois. *www.aubade.com*

Réciproque. Réciproque is a huge consignment retailer, divided into six different stores by type of clothing (women's, men's, etc.). I think the key to success here is not to get fixated on wanting something in particular — e.g., a Dior suit — because they are sure not to fit. If you find something wonderful, that's great, but it's almost as much fun just to browse through racks and racks of designer French clothing. 89, 92, 93, 95, 97, 101 rue de la Pompe. *www .reciproque.fr*

AM Studio. This is a bright and tiny store selling really reasonably priced clothing: brightly colored dresses and chic bags. I bought a pair of bright red lace-up Victorian-style boots for 130 euros. 85 boulevard Beaumarchais.

Goyard made the bag that I trailed a

...oman up an escalator to see. Their bags ...re magnificent, and the Goyard logo on the outside is hand-painted. 233 rue Saint-Honoré. *www.goyard.com*

BHV is good for all sorts of things, from children's clothing to hammers or linens. It's the Macy's of Paris and well worth exploring. Plus, they have a somewhat utilitarian but very reasonably priced cafeteria where retired people happily eat their lunches. Very good for kids. 55 rue de la Verrerie. You can easily walk to the Marais from BHV. *www.bhv.fr*

Parapluies Simon. This is an intoxicating umbrella store. Alessandro bought me a present here: a pink umbrella edged with three rows of ruffled polka-dot silk (the Minnie Mouse umbrella came from a clothing store). I feel like Julie Andrews with it, as if I might stroll into a painting and have tea with penguins, à la *Mary Poppins.* 56 boulevard Saint-Michel. *www.parapluies-simon.com*

Commelin. If you happen to have a charm bracelet (or know someone who does), this is the place to come, since they've been making charms since 1880, and you can

actually see the artisans at work. The wo[r]
shop is at 39 rue des Francs-Bourgeois. [I]
says on the website that you're supposed to
have an appointment, but we just showed
up. *www.bijouxcommelin.com*

AND FINALLY . . .

For hair emergencies (and simply great cuts
and color from someone who speaks
English), go to **StylePixie Salon.** They're
a bit tricky to find, but they give you clear
directions. 2 rue Edouard-Vasseur. *www*
.stylepixiesalon.com

ABOUT THE AUTHOR

Eloisa James (aka Mary Bly) is a Shakespeare professor at Fordham University in New York City and a *New York Times* best-selling author of historical romance novels. Visit the author's websites at www.parisin lovebook.com and www.eloisajames.com.

The employees of Thorndike Press hope you have enjoyed this Large Print book. All our Thorndike, Wheeler, and Kennebec Large Print titles are designed for easy reading, and all our books are made to last. Other Thorndike Press Large Print books are available at your library, through selected bookstores, or directly from us.

For information about titles, please call:
  (800) 223-1244

or visit our Web site at:
  http://gale.cengage.com/thorndike

To share your comments, please write:
  Publisher
  Thorndike Press
  10 Water St., Suite 310
  Waterville, ME 04901